Factorization Models for Multi-Relational Data

Factorization Models for Multi-Relational Data

A thesis submitted for the degree of
Doctor of Natural Science (Dr. rer. nat.)

by

Lucas Rêgo Drumond

Department of Computer Science

Information Systems and Machine Learning Lab (ISMLL)

UNIVERSITY OF HILDESHEIM, GERMANY

Winter 2014

Bibliografische Information der Deutschen Nationalbibliothek

Die Deutsche Nationalbibliothek verzeichnet diese Publikation in der Deutschen Nationalbibliografie; detaillierte bibliografische Daten sind im Internet über http://dnb.d-nb.de abrufbar.

1. Aufl. - Göttingen: Cuvillier, 2014

Zugl.: Hildesheim, Univ., Diss., 2014

ISBN 978-3-95404-734-5

eISBN 978-3-7369-4734-4

To my brother Rafael Drumond.

Acknowledgements

During the work that resulted on this thesis I have had the support of many people. First and foremost I want to thank my advisor Prof. Dr. Dr. Lars Schmidt-Thieme for his support, patience, insightful advice and for the many fruitful discussions throughout these years that were crucial for the development of this work.

I would also like to thank all the members of the Information Systems and Machine Learning Lab (ISMLL) at the University of Hildesheim, in particular Zeno Gantner, Steffen Rendle, Christoph Freudenthaler, Artus Krohn-Grimberghe for the close and invaluable collaboration. Also I would like to thank specially my office mate Nicolas Schilling and Josif Grabocka for the insightful comments on this thesis and for the long and fruitful discussions on related and unrelated topics from which I certainly learned a lot.

During my time as a PhD student I had the honor and the pleasure to participate in a fruitful collaboration with Ernesto Diaz-Aviles. Some of the many results of this collaboration are reflected in this thesis.

A very special thanks for my dear friend Leandro Balby Marinho, who not only inspired me to pursue an academic career, but always supported me and provided good and insightful advice.

I would like to thank DAAD and CNPq for the financial support during my PhD studies.

And last, but not least, I thank Kirsten for the understanding and support on the final days of my PhD studies and my entire family and friends, especially my brother Rafael and my parents Alberto and Celi for the unconditional support and for being my source of motivation.

Abstract

Mining multi-relational data has gained relevance in the last years and found applications in a number of tasks like recommender systems, link prediction, RDF mining, natural language processing, protein-interaction prediction and social network analysis just to cite a few. Appropriate machine learning models for such tasks must not only be able to operate on large scale scenarios, but also deal with noise, partial inconsistencies, ambiguities, or duplicate entries in the data. In recent years there has been a growing interest on multi-relational factorization models since they have shown to be a scalable and effective approach for multi-relational learning.

Although many models have been proposed for dealing with relational data, it is not trivial to discuss and compare them since the notation and terminology used differs heavily from each other depending on for which real world task they are originally applied to. We formalize the relational learning problem and rewrite state-of-the-art approaches under the proposed notational framework, thus allowing us to identify similarities between various models and gaps in the current technology.

Then, building on existing recommender systems literature for learning from positive-only implicit feedback, we investigate how to properly deal with the open world assumption present in many real world relational datasets. In particular, we analyze the impact of considering positive-only observations in the loss function for which the factorization models are optimized.

Next we investigate the problem of making predictions for multiple target relations. Early models address the problem where with only one target relation for which predictions should be made. More recent models address the multi-target variant of the problem and use the same set of parameters to make predictions for all target relations. State-of-the-art models are learned by optimizing the sum of the losses on all relations in the data thus learning parameters that offer the best performance compromise over all relations. We propose a framework for optimizing relational learning models for the best performance on each relation individually instead of the best average performance over the target relations. We also provide empirical evidence on real world datasets that this approach presents competitive results against state-of-the-art methods while being able to scale well to large amounts of data.

Finally we present an application of multi-relational models to a standard machine learning problem – namely, semi-supervised classification. We first formulate the problem as an instance of a relational learning problem and then propose a novel semi-supervised classification approach which is based on a factorization model.

Contents

List of Figures

List of Tables

Notation

This thesis will adhere to the following notational conventions:

X	a set, denoted by a capital letter
x	a variable indicating either an entity instance or a scalar
$\hat{y}$ or $\hat{y}_i$	a predicted value for a variable y
$\mathbf{X}$	a matrix, denoted by a capital bold letter
$\mathbf{X}^\top$	a transposed matrix
$\mathbf{w}$	a vector, denoted by a bold letter
$\mathbf{w}^\top$	a transposed vector
w_{ij}	an element of a matrix $\mathbf{X}$
$\varphi(x)$	a latent feature vector associated with the variable x
Φ_r	a latent feature matrix associated with the relation r
$y_r(x_1, x_2)$	the target variable value for a relation r and instances x_1 and x_2
$\hat{y}_r(x_1, x_2)$	the predicted value for atarget variable value for a relation r and instances x_1 and x_2
$\lVert \cdot \rVert_F$	The Frobenius norm
$\mathcal{X}_r$	predictor space for a relation r
$\mathcal{Y}_r$	target space for a relation r
R	the number of relations in a dataset
n_r	the arity of a relation r
$\mathcal{E}$	set of entity instances
$\mathcal{E}_r^{(1)}$	set of entity instances that can act as the subject of relation r
$\mathcal{E}_r^{(2)}$	set of entity instances that can act as the object of relation r
D_r^{train}	the training data for a relation r
D_r^{test}	the test data for a relation r

Abbreviation

BPR	Bayesian Personalized Ranking
CATSMF	Coupled Auxiliary and Target Specific Matrix Factorization
CD	Canonical Decomposition
CMF	Collective Matrix Factorization
DMF	Decoupled Matrix Factorization
kNN	k-Nearest Neighbors
LOD	Linked Open Data
MF	Matrix Factorization
MOF-SRP	Multiple Order Factorization with Shared Relation Parameters
MRMF	Multi-Relational Matrix Factorization
MrWTD	Multi-Relational Weighted Tensor Factorization
NNMF	Non-Negative Multiple Matrix Factorization
PITF	Pairwise Interaction Tensor Factorization
PNT-CMF	Predictor/Neighborhood/Target Collective Matrix Factorization
RDF	Resource Description Framework
RESCAL	RESCAL
RMSE	Root Mean Squared Error
SGD	Stochastic Gradient Descent
SME	Semantic Matching Energy
SRL	Statistical Relational Learning

Chapter 1

Introduction

Contents

Statistical Relational Learning (SRL) has proved successful to learn efficiently from the large amount of interlinked information available, for instance on the Web. SRL approaches are capable to deal with the inherent noise of large heterogeneous relational datasets, which includes partial inconsistencies, ambiguities, or duplicate entities. Factorization models have proven to be powerful models for relational learning, providing highly competitive prediction performance while being able to scale to large dataset sizes. However, new paradigms are still needed towards statistical and computational inference based on relational data.

1.1 Multi-relational learning

Statistical machine learning models (Hastie *et al.*, 2009) assume that data points in a dataset are all sampled independently from each other but from the same distribution, which is known as the independent and identically distributed (iid) assumption and that data instances are represented as points in a high-dimensional space. This largely simplifies statistical inference and has enabled many practical applications of machine learning models However. One of its implications is that the models are able to exploit attribute information about the instances but ignores any information about the relationships between them. However many real world datasets contain rich relational structure and knowing how different data points are related, does provide useful information about them. For instance, when predicting the topic of a Web document, it is useful to know the topics of the documents it is connected to through hyperlinks; also, in a social network environment, the interests of the friends of a given user, are a good indicator of his/her own interests. To see how this is important, take as an example the task of predicting the blood type of a person. Knowing the blood type of a person x does not provide a priori any information about the blood type of another person y. However if it is known that x is the father of y, then the blood type of x does provide some indication on the likely blood type of y. In statistical terms, let P be a probability distribution, $B(x) \in \{a, b, o\}$ a variable denoting the blood type of x and $F(x, y) \in \{0, 1\}$ a variable denoting whether x is the father of y. Then, for a typical iid model,

$$P(B(y)|B(x)) = P(B(y))$$

since the model assumes that $B(y)$ and $B(x)$ are independently sampled.

A relational model is a model capable of considering relationships between instances like the `father-of` relation denoted by the variable $F(x, y)$. Since the blood type is a genetic characteristic, knowing that $F(x, y) = 1$ means that $B(y)$ and $B(x)$ are not independent anymore:

$$P(B(y)|B(x), F(x, y) = 1) \neq P(B(y)) \ .$$

This of course models the data in a better way. The independence assumption of iid models makes it easier to compute the joint distribution $P(B(x), B(y))$:

$$P(B(x), B(y)|F(x, y)) = P(B(x)|F(x, y))P(B(y)|F(x, y)) = P(B(x))P(B(y))$$

whereas for the relational model the joint distribution is given by:

$$P(B(x), B(y), F(x, y)) = P(B(y)|B(x), F(x, y))P(B(x)|F(x, y))P(F(x, y)) \ .$$

Note that instead of simply multiplying the marginals $P(B(x))$ and $P(B(y))$, the conditionals have to be defined and computed. This difference might not look big on this toy example but for moderate scale datasets it might render such distribution infeasible to represent and compute. The challenge is to design a model that compactly represents information like $F(x, y)$ for a large dataset. Also the conditionals $P(B(y)|B(x), F(x,y))$ and $P(B(x)|F(x,y))$ need to be defined, as well as scalable strategies to learn their parameters and make inference about them. This is sensible in real world datasets because a single entity instance can be related to a number of different instances through a variety of relationships. To have an idea of how crucial this is for machine learning models let us take a look at a simple likelihood function of a parameter vector Θ given a dataset $\mathcal{D}$. The likelihood can be written as:

$$\mathcal{L}(\Theta|\mathcal{D}) = P(\mathcal{D}|\Theta)P(\Theta) = \left(\prod_{d \in \mathcal{D}} P(d|\Theta) \right) P(\Theta) \, .$$

The probability $P(\mathcal{D}|\Theta)$ could only be simplified in the product above because of the iid assumption on the data points $d \in \mathcal{D}$. Assume now that we have a non-iid dataset $\mathcal{D} = \{d_1, d_2, d_3\}$, then $P(\mathcal{D}|\Theta)$ is now:

$$P(\mathcal{D}|\Theta) = P(d_1|d_2, d_3, \Theta)P(d_2|d_3, \Theta)P(d_3|\Theta)$$

One can easily see that, for a small dataset it is infeasible to compute the likelihood. From this discussion, two basic problems arise when dealing with relational data: (i) how to compactly represent a joint distribution of model and data with relational information and (ii) develop models for which inference is feasible.

The first problem was originally approached by using first order logic as a representation formalism (Muggleton & De Raedt, 1994). The Inductive Logic Programming (Muggleton & De Raedt, 1994) is a general approach to learn first order logic inference rules from relational databases.

While this approach has the advantage that the models are easily interpretable and understandable by humans, it has the drawback that logic based methods are not able to deal with incomplete or noisy data. This seriously limits their application to real world problems. In order to overcome this problem, Statistical Relational Learning (SRL) models (Friedman *et al.*, 1999; Getoor & Taskar, 2007; Kersting, 2006; Neville *et al.*, 2003) combine knowledge representation formalisms like first-order logic with probabilistic graphical models. A number SRL models have been proposed like the Bayesian Logic Programs (Kersting, 2006) and the Markov Logic Networks (Richardson & Domingos, 2006). At the same time, non-parametric bayesian approaches like IRM (Kemp *et al.*, 2006) and IHRM (Xu *et al.*, 2006) have been proposed for relational learning.

1.1.1 Factorization models for Multi-relational data

Although powerful, general and expressive, SRL models still suffer from scalability issues. Recently, multi-relational factorization models have shown to scale well while providing good predictive performance and are currently considered as the state-of-the-art for SRL tasks (Jenatton *et al.*, 2012; Nickel *et al.*, 2011; Singh & Gordon, 2008b). Factorization models for multi-relational data associate entities and relations with latent feature vectors and define predictions about new relationships through operations on these vectors (e.g., dot products). Nickel *et al.* (2011) showed that these models are strongly competitive against MLNs while they have much better scalability. Singh & Gordon (2010) provide some insight about why factorization models work well with relational data. Basically, a factorization model assumes that data points are a priori related and that they are only independent given the latent features. Using the bayes theorem this results in a model which considers relationships between entities in the data but can also be learned using the machinery developed for models under the iid assumption. To be more clear, in the blood type example, a factorization model would assign latent features $\varphi(x), \varphi(y)$ to x and y respectively. Given the latent features the blood types of both instances are independent:

$$P(B(y)|B(x), \varphi(y), F(x, y)) = P(B(y)|\varphi(y))$$

The latent features φ can be easily computed, for instance by maximum likelihood estimators based on the relational data. Since the data points are independent given the latent features, it is true that $P(\mathcal{D}|\varphi) = \prod_{d \in \mathcal{D}} P(d|\varphi)$.

Although vastly studied, most of the work on factorization models for relational learning focused on how the prediction function looks like, i.e. whether to consider three or two way interactions (Jenatton *et al.*, 2012), which kind of latent features to employ, e.g. whether to use feature vectors or matrices (Nickel *et al.*, 2011) or the usage of only non-negative features (Takeuchi *et al.*, 2013), whether to use link functions (London *et al.*, 2012) and so on. Other aspects of the relational learning problem were either not considered or not yet fully investigated. For instance, most of the available relational data come only with positive observations. Since usually machine learning models need both positive and negative examples for training, this issue needs to be closely examined. Another aspect not fully addressed is the fact that in most of the multi-relational learning tasks, predictions are to be made for multiple target relations. State-of-the-art models are optimized for a loss that is the (weighted) sum of the losses on each relation. How to carefully optimize each relation individually is still an open issue. This thesis discusses how the state-of-the-art factorization models look like, identifies open problems in the field and approach them in a principled way.

1.1.2 Applications of Multi Relational Learning

One question that can be asked is: is there enough relational information available so that it is worth to develop models capable of exploiting such data in large scales? The answer is yes. Mining multi-relational data with noise, partial inconsistencies, ambiguities, or duplicate entities, has gained relevance in the last years and found applications in a number of tasks. There is a plethora of datasets containing relational information, especially on the Web. One prominent example is the Semantic Web Semantic Web's Linked Open Data (LOD) initiative where the data consists of triples containing a predicate relating a subject and an object. Example of large LOD bases are DBpedia[1] and YAGO (Suchanek *et al.*, 2007). The task of **LOD mining** can be useful for statistically querying such databases (Drumond *et al.*, 2012) and for predicting new triples (Drumond *et al.*, 2012; Nickel *et al.*, 2012).

Another broad application area for relational learning methods are **recommender systems** (Koren *et al.*, 2009). The task of recommender systems can be seen as the prediction of a relation between users and items. Often, additional relational side information about users is available such as friendship relationship between them and about items, such as, for instance, which movies share the same director. This additional information can be exploited by multi-relational models for improving the recommendation performance (Lippert *et al.*, 2008; Singh & Gordon, 2008b) or for alleviating cold-start problems (Krohn-Grimberghe *et al.*, 2012).

Natural language processing is another field where the datasets available contain lots of relational information. For instance, relationships between words like the subject and object of a verb can be predicted using multi-relational models (Jenatton *et al.*, 2012; McCray, 2003). Other example of tasks involving relational data are **protein-interaction prediction** (Lippert *et al.*, 2008), **mining of geopolitical information** (Rummel, 1999) and **entity linking** (Shen *et al.*, 2012).

---

[1] http://dbpedia.org/

1.2 Contribution

Although a number of relational models have been proposed in the last years, there are still gaps in the state-of-the-art which need to be investigated. The main goal of this thesis is to provide a cohesive view of the state-of-the-art, identify such gaps and propose solutions to close them. Specifically, our contributions are summarized as follows:

- **Formalize the relational learning problem and study the state-of-the-art under a single notational framework.** We propose a formalization for representing multi-relational data and the multi-relational learning problem. State-of-the-art models are described under a single notational framework which makes it possible to identify redundancies (similar or equivalent models) and open problems not yet properly addressed in the literature.

- **Study the problem of learning from positive only data in the context of multi-relational models.** We investigate the impact of explicitly considering the open-world semantics of many datasets in the loss function. We argue why the evaluation protocols usually used in the literature are not suitable for evaluating models on data with only positive observations and propose a more suitable evaluation procedure. We also adapt approaches from the item recommendation community to the multi-relational learning problem and evaluate them.

- **Propose a new approach for learning models for multiple target relations.** A new factorization approach that optimizes directly for a number of target relations is proposed. We argue that the models should be optimized for the best performance on each relation individually. We show how this approach can improve state-of-the-art performance.

- **Apply multi-relational factorization models to semi-supervised binary classification.** The semi-supervised classification problem is formalized as a multi-relational learning problem using our proposed notational framework. We propose a new semi-supervised classification approach, namely PNT-CMF, a factorization model that collectively factorizes the predictor, neighborhood and target relation and devise a learning algorithm for it.

- **Empirical evaluation and analysis**. The proposed methods are evaluated using both small and large publicly available data sets. The proposed methods are compared against state-of-the-art methods. We empirically show that, in most of the cases, the proposed methods can achieve better prediction performance than their competitors and scale to large problems.

1.3 Submitted and Published Work

The contributions of this thesis were published in international conferences. The list of publications is as follows:

- Lucas Drumond, Steffen Rendle and Lars Schmidt-Thieme (2012). *Predicting RDF triples in incomplete knowledge bases with tensor factorization.* In Proceedings of the 27th Annual ACM Symposium on Applied Computing, SAC 12, 326331, Riva Del Garda, Italy.

  The content of this paper is mostly covered in Chapter 3.

- Lucas Drumond, Lars Schmidt-Thieme, Christoph Freudenthaler and Artus Krohn- Grimberghe (2014). *Collective Matrix Factorization of Predictors, Neighbor- hood and Targets for Semi-Supervised Classification.* In Proceedings of the 18th Pacific-Asia Conference on Knowledge Discovery and Data Mining, PAKDD 2014, 286297, Tainan, Taiwan.

  The content of this paper is covered in Chapter 5.

Also the following paper, which covers the content of Chapter 4, is under the revision process for publication:

- Lucas Drumond, Lars Schmidt-Thieme, Ernesto Diaz-Aviles. Optimizing Multi-Relational Factorization Models for Multiple Target Relations. *submitted.*

During the time of my doctoral studies I co-authored further publications that, although not covered in this thesis, are related to or have influenced the work presented here.

- Josif Grabocka, Lucas Drumond, Lars Schmidt-Thieme (2013): Supervised Dimensionality Reduction Via Nonlinear Target Estimation, in Proceedings of the 15th International Conference on Data Warehousing and Knowledge Discovery, DaWaK 2013.

- Nguyen Thai-Nghe, Lucas Drumond, Tomáš Horváth, Lars Schmidt-Thieme (2012): Using factorization machines for student modeling, in Workshop and Poster Proceedings of the 20th Conference on User Modeling, Adaptation, and Personalization, Montreal, Canada.

- Ernesto Diaz-Aviles, Lucas Drumond, Zeno Gantner, Lars Schmidt-Thieme, Wolfgang Nejdl (2012): What is Happening Right Now ... That Interests Me? Online Topic Discovery and Recommendation in Twitter , Proceedings of the 21st ACM International Conference on Information and Knowledge Management (CIKM 2012).

- Ernesto Diaz-Aviles, Lucas Drumond, Lars Schmidt-Thieme, Wolfgang Nejdl (2012): Real-Time Top-N Recommendation within Social Streams , Proceedings of the 6th ACM International Conference on Recommender Systems (RecSys'12).

- Zeno Gantner, Lucas Drumond, Christoph Freudenthaler, Lars Schmidt-Thieme (2012): Personalized Ranking for Non-Uniformly Sampled Items, Journal of Machine Learning Research Workshop and Conference Proceedings.

- Artus Krohn-Grimberghe, Lucas Drumond, Christoph Freudenthaler, Lars Schmidt-Thieme (2012): Multi-Relational Matrix Factorization using Bayesian Personalized Ranking for Social Network Data , Proceedings of the Fifth ACM International Conference on Web Search and Data Mining.

- Zeno Gantner, Lucas Drumond, Christoph Freudenthaler, Lars Schmidt-Thieme (2011): Bayesian Personalized Ranking for Non-Uniformly Sampled Items, in KDD Cup Workshop 2011, San Diego, USA.

- Nguyen Thai-Nghe, Lucas Drumond, Tomáš Horváth, Lars Schmidt-Thieme (2011): Multi-Relational Factorization Models for Predicting Student Performance, in KDD 2011 Workshop on Knowledge Discovery in Educational Data (KDDinED 2011). Held as part of the 17th ACM SIGKDD Conference on Knowledge Discovery and Data Mining.

- Timo Reuter, Philipp Cimiano, Lucas Drumond, Krisztian Buza, Lars Schmidt-Thieme (2011): Scalable event-based clustering of social media via record linkage techniques, in Fifth International AAAI Conference on Weblogs and Social Media.

- Nguyen Thai-Nghe, Lucas Drumond, Tomáš Horváth, Artus Krohn-Grimberghe, Alexandros Nanopoulos, Lars Schmidt-Thieme (2011): Factorization Techniques for Predicting Student Performance, to appear in Educational Recommender Systems and Technologies: Practices and Challenges (ERSAT 2011): Santos, O. C. and Boticario, J. G. (Eds.), IGI Global.

- Nguyen Thai-Nghe, Lucas Drumond, Tomáš Horváth, Alexandros Nanopoulos, Lars Schmidt-Thieme (2011): Matrix and Tensor Factorization for Predicting Student Performance, in Proceedings of the 3rd International Conference on Computer Supported Education (CSEDU 2011). Best Student Paper Award.

- Zeno Gantner, Lucas Drumond, Christoph Freudenthaler, Steffen Rendle, Lars Schmidt-Thieme (2010): Learning Attribute-to-Feature Mappings for Cold-Start Recommendations, in Proceedings of the 10th IEEE International Conference on Data Mining (ICDM 2010), Sydney, Australia.

- Nguyen Thai-Nghe, Lucas Drumond, Artus Krohn-Grimberghe, Lars Schmidt-Thieme (2010): Recommender System for Predicting Student Performance, in Proceedings of ACM RecSys 2010 Workshop on Recommender Systems for Technology Enhanced Learning (RecSysTEL 2010), Elsevier Computer Science Procedia, pp. 2811-2819.

1.4 Chapter Overview

The thesis is organized as follows:

- In **Chapter 2** a formalization for the relational learning problem is proposed and the state-of-the-art is discussed and rewritten under the proposed formalization. This allowed to identify similarities between various models and gaps in the current technology.

- **Chapter 3** investigates the impact of considering positive only observations on the loss function. It builds on previous work from the recommender systems literature on learning from positive only instances (Rendle *et al.*, 2009a) and further investigates this issue on LOD datasets.

- A new framework for multi-relational learning is proposed in **Chapter 4**. This chapter investigates the problem of making predictions for multiple relations and proposes to employ a different set of parameters in the prediction function per target relation, so that the model can be optimized for the best performance on each relation individually instead of the best average performance over the target relations.

- **Chapter 5** presents an application of multi-relational factorization models to a standard machine learning problem, namely semi-supervised classification. The problem is formulated as an instance of a relational learning problem and a new semi-supervised classification model is proposed, which is based on a factorization model. Experiments on real world datasets show that the model outperforms state-of-the-art semi-supervised classifiers.

- Finally, **Chapter 6** puts all the proposed methods into context for comparison and conclusion. We also give an outlook in this area and raise some works for the future.

Chapter 2

The Multi-Relational Factorization Problem

Contents

Learning from relational data has a multitude of possible applications ranging from protein-interaction prediction (Lippert *et al.*, 2008) to social network analysis (Krohn-Grimberghe *et al.*, 2012). These different applications in general correspond to standard machine learning problems like regression, classification and learning to rank. The difference between relational data and standard attribute based data is that, in the former, information about how the data points relate to each other is available. For instance, in a social network application, not only user attributes are known but also with which other users he/she is connected, e.g. through a friendship relationship. Although many machine learning models proposed for dealing with relational data have a lot in common, it is not trivial to discuss and compare them since the notation and terminology used by each paper differs heavily from each other depending on for which real world task they are proposed. In this chapter a formal description of the relational learning problem that is general enough to describe the problems addressed in this thesis is provided. After that, state-of-the-art factorization models for multi-relational data are discussed and described under the proposed notational framework.

2.1 Problem Formulation

Relational Data

Relational data comprise a set of $R \in \mathbb{N}$ relations among a set of entities $\mathcal{E}$. The data for a given relation $r \in \{1, \ldots, R\}$ can be described as $D_r := \{(e_r, y_r) | e_r \in E_r \wedge y_r \in \mathbb{R}\}$ where $E_r \subseteq \mathcal{E}^{n_r}$ is called the *extension* of relation r and n_r denotes its arity. y_r is a value associated with each observation.

Many times y_r denotes the truth value of a given observation and can be encoded as $y_r \in \{0, 1\}$. As an example, imagine a binary relation relating countries to their capitals. Possible observations could be $(\text{Germany}, \text{Berlin}, 1)$ and $(\text{Germany}, \text{Hamburg}, 0)$. Also y_r can assume other kinds of values depending on the semantics of the relation. For instance, in a recommender system it may indicate the rating that a user gave to an item. In this case, possible observations would be $(\text{John}, \text{The Matrix}, 3)$ and $(\text{John}, \text{The Godfather}, 5)$.

The Learning Problem

The problem posed by relational data is to learn models to predict y_r values given e_r and, possibly, some additional information. Let $\mathcal{X}_r, \mathcal{Y}_r$ be sets called predictor and target spaces of relation r, respectively, for $r = 1, \ldots, R$. Later on it will be discussed how $\mathcal{X}_r$ and $\mathcal{Y}_r$ look like in real world problems. For now assume that $\mathcal{X}_r := E_r$ and $\mathcal{Y}_r := \mathbb{R}$. This way, the training data for a relation r can be written as $D_r^{\text{train}} \subseteq \mathcal{X}_r \times \mathcal{Y}_r$.

Let $Y_r = \{\hat{y}_r : \mathcal{X}_r \to \mathcal{Y}_r\}$ be the space of all possible prediction models considered and $L_r : \mathcal{P}(\mathcal{X}_r \times \mathcal{Y}_r) \times Y_r \to \mathbb{R}_0^+$ be a loss function, where $\mathcal{P}$ denotes the power set. Given the training data, the multi-relational multi-target prediction problem is to find R models $\hat{y}_r : \mathcal{X}_r \to \mathcal{Y}_r$ s.t. for some test data $D_r^{\text{test}} \subseteq \mathcal{X}_r \times \mathcal{Y}_r$ $(r = 1, \ldots, R)$ stemming from the same data generating process as the training data and not being used for learning the models $\hat{y}_r$, the test error

$$\text{error}((D_r^{\text{test}})_{r=1,\dots,R}, (\hat{y}_r)_{r=1,\dots,R}) := \frac{1}{R} \sum_{r=1}^{R} L_r(D_r^{\text{test}}, \hat{y}_r)$$

is minimal.

For regression and classification problems, losses L_r usually are defined as in Equation 2.1.

$$L_r(D_r^{\text{test}}, \hat{y}_r) := \frac{1}{|D_r^{\text{test}}|} \sum_{(x,y) \in D_r^{\text{test}}} \ell_r(y, \hat{y}_r(x)) \tag{2.1}$$

Equation 2.1 is a sum of pointwise losses

$$\ell_r : \mathcal{Y}_r \times \mathcal{Y}_r \to \mathbb{R}_0^+$$

such as the squared error $\ell_r(y, \hat{y}_r) := (y - \hat{y})^2$ or the misclassification rate $\ell_r(y, \hat{y}_r) := \delta(y \neq \hat{y})$ where $\delta(A) := 1$, if A is true and $\delta(A) := 0$ otherwise.

Many multi-relational datasets consist of positive instances only, e.g., the tuples of entities $\mathcal{E}$ in a subset of the extension of the relation. This means that we only observe a subset of the tuples of the type (x, y) where $y = 1$. In this case we are interested in solving a ranking task where prediction functions $Y_r = \{\hat{y}_r : \mathcal{X}_r \to \mathbb{R}\}$ deliver ranking scores and the losses L_r usually are defined pairwise:

$$L_r(D_r^{\text{test}}, \hat{y}_r) := \frac{1}{|D_r^{\text{test}}||\mathcal{X}_r \times \{1\} \setminus (D_r^{\text{train}} \cup D_r^{\text{test}})|} \sum_{(x,1) \in D_r^{\text{test}}} \tag{2.2}$$

$$\sum_{(x',1) \in \mathcal{X}_r \times \{1\} \setminus (D_r^{\text{train}} \cup D_r^{\text{test}})} \ell_r(\hat{y}_r(x), \hat{y}_r(x'))$$

with pair ranking score losses

$$\ell_r : \mathbb{R} \times \mathbb{R} \to \mathbb{R}_0^+$$

such as 0/1 loss for incorrectly ranked pairs $\ell_r(\hat{y}(x), \hat{y}(x')) := \delta(\hat{y}(x) < \hat{y}(x'))$. Here, x is a positive example, x' a negative example and $1 - L_r$ becomes the area under the ROC curve (AUC) .

Throughout this thesis we assume the relations we are dealing with to be binary, i.e., they have arity 2. For such relations, the predictor and the target spaces $\mathcal{X}_r, \mathcal{Y}_r$ are defined as:

$$\mathcal{X}_r := \mathcal{E} \times \mathcal{E}$$
$$\mathcal{Y}_r := \mathbb{R}.$$

For a given observation $(x_1, x_2) \in \mathcal{X}_r$, x_1 and x_2 are usually called subject and object respectively, and the loss L_r in Equation 2.2 compares only to negative examples x' with the same subject $x'_1 = x_1$. For large entity sets $\mathcal{E}$, L_r usually is not computed for all negative examples, but just for a sample of fixed size. Finally, problems with additional entity type information can be modeled by choosing $\mathcal{X}_r := \mathcal{E}_r^{(1)} \times \mathcal{E}_r^{(2)}$ with $\mathcal{E}_r^{(1)} \subseteq \mathcal{E}$ and $\mathcal{E}_r^{(2)} \subseteq \mathcal{E}$ being subsets of entities that can possibly be related through relation r as subjects and objects respectively.

2.2 State of the Art

Statistical Relational Learning (SRL) (Getoor & Taskar, 2007) aims at statistically modeling relational data. Early work on SRL combines graphical models such as Bayesian and Markov networks, with knowledge representation formalisms such as first order logic for an accurate modeling of the relationships (Kersting, 2006; Richardson & Domingos, 2006). Another approach to SRL is multi-relational factorization models, which embed entities into a latent space and reconstruct the relations through operations on this space. State-of-the-art factorization models may differ in two different key aspects: (i) how they are parametrized and (ii) how the parameters are learned. In order to illustrate the concepts discussed in this section we use a running example of a social media website where users can follow other users (much like in Twitter), be friends with other users (like in an online social network) and consume products, e.g., read news items. In this example there are two entity types, namely users U and news items N and three relations: follows $F := U \times U$, the social relationship $S := U \times U$ and the product consumption (reading of news items) $C := U \times N$. This section discusses the different existing parametrizations as well as learning strategies, mostly from the point of view of which loss functions they are optimized for.

2.2.1 Parametrization of Multi-relational factorization models

Latent Factor models define a mapping $\varphi : \mathcal{E} \to \mathbb{R}^k$ associating latent features with every entity $x \in \mathcal{E}$, with $k \in \mathbb{N}$ being the number of latent features. Prediction functions are often defined as operations in this latent feature space. Early models like the Multi-Relational Matrix Factorization (MRMF) from Lippert *et al.* (2008) and the Collective Matrix Factorization (CMF) from Singh & Gordon (2008b) use the following prediction function:

$$\hat{y}_r(x_1, x_2) := \varphi(x_1)^\top \varphi(x_2) \tag{2.3}$$

We note that the same model was proposed 5 years later under the name of Non-Negative Multiple Matrix Factorization (NNMF) (Takeuchi *et al.*, 2013). The only difference between NNMF and CMF is that the former poses a non-negativity constraint on the latent features. This bilinear model has the advantage of the computational ease but can poorly handle relations with a signature clash, i.e., different relations between the same entity types like the *friends* and *follows* relation from our example. For instance such a model would predict that every user who follows *Barack Obama* is also a friend of him.

One way to cope with this issue is to associate feature matrices $\Phi_r \in \mathbb{R}^{k \times k}$ with each relation:

$$\hat{y}_r(x_1, x_2) := \varphi(x_1)^\top \Phi_r \varphi(x_2) \tag{2.4}$$

If the relation features Φ_r are diagonal matrices, this model is equivalent to a PARAFAC tensor decomposition (Harshman, 1970). The Semantic Matching Energy (SME) model (Glorot *et al.*, 2013) also uses this approach although with a slightly different prediction function. This solves the signature clash issue but another limitation remains. For diagonal or any other kind of symmetric matrices Φ_r, one can easily see that, for the models from Equation 2.3 and Equation 2.4, $\hat{y}_r(x_1, x_2) = \hat{y}_r(x_2, x_1)$. This is an issue when dealing with asymmetric relations, i.e., relations where $y(x_1, x_2) \neq y(x_2, x_1)$ like the *follows* relation in our example. In this case the model would predict that *Barack Obama* is interested in following every user that follows him, which is not necessarily true.

Using full asymmetric matrices for Φ_r yields a model capable of dealing with this problem. This is the prediction model used by RESCAL (Nickel *et al.*, 2011) and has proven to be a strong approach, performing well on different scenatios. The disadvantage of this model is that it comes at the expense of computational cost, both from processing time and memory standpoints. Jenatton *et al.* (2012)

propose a model that aims at reducing the memory requirements by defining relation features as outer products of feature vectors. This means that the relation features are still full matrices which in turn are factorized so that they can be stored with more modest memory requirements. Also, unlike RESCAL, their model considers both pairwise and three-wise interactions between entities and relations when reconstructing the tensor. Another feature of this model is that it reduces the number of parameters by sharing features across relations. This is done by defining the relation feature matrices Φ_r as the outer product of shared low rank latent feature vectors. Since no specific name has been given to this model by its authors, we will refer to it model as the Multiple Order Factorization with Shared Relation Parameters (MOF-SRP)[1]. The prediction function for MOF-SRP is given by Equation 2.5.

$$\hat{y}_r^{MOF-SRP}(x_1, x_2) := \mathbf{a}\Phi_r\mathbf{a}^\top + \varphi(x_1)\Phi_r\mathbf{b}^\top + \mathbf{b}\Phi_r\varphi(x_2)^\top + \varphi(x_1)^\top\Phi_r\varphi(x_2) \quad (2.5)$$

$$\Phi_r = \sum_{j=1}^{d} w_j^r \mathbf{u}_j \mathbf{v}_j^\top$$

There, $\mathbf{w}^r \in \mathbb{R}^d$ is a sparse vector, $\mathbf{u}_j, \mathbf{v}_j \in \mathbb{R}^k$ are the relation latent parameters, and $\mathbf{a}, \mathbf{b} \in \mathbb{R}^k$ are parameter vectors.

Localized Matrix Factorization (LMF) (Agarwal *et al.*, 2011) also uses dense matrices as relation features, that although slightly differently parametrized, can be shown to be equivalent to RESCAL. LMF associates each instance with a feature vector $\varphi(x) \in \mathbb{R}^k$ and feature mappings for different relations. Each relation has two feature mappings, one for its subjects $\Phi_{r,0} \in \mathbb{R}^{k \times k}$ and one for the objects $\Phi_{r,1} \in \mathbb{R}^{k \times k}$. This means that the features that LMF uses to make a prediction for a relation r are

$$\Phi_{r,0}\varphi(x)$$

for its subjects and

$$\Phi_{r,1}\varphi(x)$$

for its objects. Then, the prediction function is given by

$$\hat{y}_r^{LMF}(x_1, x_2) := b_{x_2}^r + (\Phi_{r,0}\varphi(x_1))^\top(\Phi_{r,1}\varphi(x_2))$$
$$= b_{x_2}^r + \varphi(x_1)^\top\Phi_{r,0}^\top\Phi_{r,1}\varphi(x_2) \quad (2.6)$$

---

[1]The authors refer to the model as a multiple order factorization (Jenatton *et al.*, 2012).

with $b^r_{x_2} \in \mathbb{R}$ being a bias term. Although this prediction function is suitable for the specific case investigated by Agarwal *et al.* (2011), when formalizing for the general multi-factorization case as done here, it can be seen that this is equivalent to RESCAL if one uses

$$\Phi_r = \Phi^\top_{r,0}\Phi_{r,1}$$

and adds the bias term. This overparametrization may render LMF more prone to overfitting and harder to optimize without any expected improvements on prediction quality in comparison to the RESCAL variant.

An extension and generalization of RESCAL was proposed by London *et al.* (2012) and is called Multi-Relational Weighted Tensor Factorization (MrWTD). MrWTD extends RESCAL in four ways: (i) it formalizes the model independent of the loss function it is optimized for; (ii) it adds a relation specific bias to the prediction function; (iii) it wraps the prediction function within a link function; and (iv) it accounts for specific observation weights. Thus the prediction function for MrWTD is given by equation 2.7.

$$\hat{y}^{MrWTD}_r(x_1, x_2) := \gamma(b_r + \varphi(x_1)^\top \Phi_r \varphi(x_2)) \tag{2.7}$$

Here $\gamma : \mathbb{R} \to \mathbb{R}$ is a link function which can be chosen according to the application. Examples of possible choices for the link function are the sign, the identity and the sigmoid function.

A slightly different approach is proposed by Bordes *et al.* (2013). They define the prediction function in two stages. First the relation features and the features of the subject combined should approximate the features of the object such that:

$$\varphi(x_1) + \Phi_r \approx \varphi(x_2)$$

for $(x_1, x_2, 1) \in D^{\mathrm{train}}_r$ and $\Phi_r \in \mathbb{R}^k$. Thus the prediction function is given by the distance between the vectors given by $\varphi(x_1) + \Phi_r$ and $\varphi(x_2)$, and the prediction function can be written as in equation 2.8.

$$\hat{y}_r(x_1, x_2) := d(\varphi(x_1) + \Phi_r, \varphi(x_2)) \tag{2.8}$$

There, $d : \mathbb{R}^k \times \mathbb{R}^k \to \mathbb{R}$ is some dissimilarity metric on $\mathbb{R}^k$ like, for instance, the euclidean distance. Since the prediction model is a dissimilarity function it behaves differently from the other models discussed here: the higher the value, the less likely the observation is to be true.

A summary of models, including the parametrization of their prediction functions, can be found in Table 2.1.

Table 2.1: **Summary of state-of-the-art multi-relational factorization models regarding their parametrization.**

Method	Prediction function $\hat{y}_r(x_1, x_2)$	Relation features
MRMF	$\varphi(x_1)^\top \varphi(x_2)$	none
CMF	$\varphi(x_1)^\top \varphi(x_2)$	none
RESCAL	$\varphi(x_1)^\top \Phi_r \varphi(x_2)$	full matrix
SME	$(\mathbf{W}_s\varphi(x_1)^\top + \mathbf{W}_s\Phi_r^\top + \mathbf{B}_s)^\top + (\mathbf{W}_o\varphi(x_2)^\top + \mathbf{W}_o\Phi_r^\top + \mathbf{B}_o)^\top$	diagonal matrix
MOF-SRP	$\mathbf{a}\Phi_r\mathbf{a}^\top + \varphi(x_1)\Phi_r\mathbf{b}^\top + \mathbf{b}\Phi_r\varphi(x_2)^\top + \varphi(x_1)^\top \Phi_r\varphi(x_2)$	$\Phi_r = \sum_{j=1}^{d} w_j^r \mathbf{u}_j \mathbf{v}_j^\top$
LMF	$\varphi(x_1)^\top \Phi_{r,0}^\top \Phi_{r,1}\varphi(x_2)$	$\Phi_r = \Phi_{r,0}^\top \Phi_{r,1}$
MrWTD	$\gamma(b_r + \varphi(x_1)^\top \Phi_r\varphi(x_2))$	full matrix

2.2.2 Optimization objectives for multi-relational learning

Each of the prediction models described above can be optimized for various loss functions. How to choose for which specific loss function to optimize the model depends heavily on the application at hand. There are however some issues with the parameter learning process that are common to all multi-relational models. They will be discussed here as well as different approaches on how to tackle them.

Historically, the first factorization models for multi-relational learning were concerned with making predictions for a single *target* relation based on information provided by a set of other relations which we refer to as *auxiliary*. The parameters are learned by optimizing the sum over the losses on each relation. In this way, the minimization of the loss on the auxiliary relations acts as a regularization term for the parameters. Singh & Gordon (2008b) formulate their CMF model as a unified view of such approaches where the overall loss is then a weighted sum of losses and the parameters are learned by optimizing the following loss function:

$$f(\Theta) := \sum_{r=1}^{R} \alpha_r L_r(D_r, \hat{y}_r(D_r; \Theta)) + Reg(\Theta) \tag{2.9}$$

where $\alpha_r \in \mathbb{R}_0^+$ is a hyperparameter for the contribution of the reconstruction of r to the overall loss and $Reg(\Theta)$ is some penalty function used to regularize the parameters Θ. A common choice for the penalty function is the Tikhonov regularization:

$$Reg(\Theta) := \lambda ||\Theta||_F^2$$

where λ is the regularization constant for the model parameters Θ and $|| \cdot ||_F$ is the Frobenius norm. As already observed in previous work (Ermis *et al.*, 2012; Krohn-Grimberghe *et al.*, 2012; Singh & Gordon, 2008b), if there is a single target relation t, better results are achieved by having a weighted sum over the losses. The idea behind this is that different relations contain useful information about the others. For instance, in the social network example from the beginning of the section, knowing which other users a given user follows might give some indication of which kind of news she is interested in. Each weight α_r models how much each relation contributes for the prediction of the target one. For instance, CMF, MrWTD and LMF use relation weights. A specific characteristic of MrWTD is that the weights on the loss function are not relation specific but rather observation specific. Since such weights should be set by the user, they are in most real world scenarios set to a constant non-negative value (usually 1) for observations in the relations and 0 for possible outcomes not observed in the data.

One issue with using relation weights however is that they are hyperparameters that need to be carefully adjusted. For a moderate number of relations, adjusting the α_r values might be infeasible through usual hyperparameter search techniques like grid search. Because of that, many models like MRMF, SME, RESCAL, and MOF-SRP simply do not weight the relations, i.e., they set $\alpha_r = 1$ for all $r = 1, \ldots, R$. One of the first attempts to learn such parameters automatically was made by Simsekli *et al.* (2013). They extended the Generalized Coupled Tensor Factorization (GCTF) model from Yilmaz (2012) with relation weights which are modeled via Exponential Dispersion models (Jorgensen, 1997). The drawback of this approach is that it is specific to their model and to specific choices of probability distributions for the relation weights, being hard to generalize to other methods.

Finally, one last issue is how to deal with different kinds of data. In some cases the relations are real valued functions of the entities involved, like for instance, in a recommender system, the rating given by a user to an item. Models optimized for the squared-loss, like MRMF and RESCAL, can cope well with this kind of problems. In other cases, the relations are binary valued functions indicating whether or not a pair of entities are related by a given relation. This is the scenario assumed by models like MOF-SRP and SME. The CMF the MrWTD models are formalized with the flexibility of using different loss functions. Similarly and independently of MrWTD another extension of RESCAL, called RESCAL-Logit , has been developed that optimizes the model for a logistic loss function (Nickel & Tresp, 2013). The learning of the parameters is performed via the L-BFGS algorithm. The authors claim that their proposed algorithm has very limited scalability. This is mostly due to the fact that the gradients used in their algorithm require the computation of a full reconstruction of each relation matrix. This could be avoided by using more memory efficient algorithms like stochastic gradient descent.

The issue with these approaches is that they assume that both positive and negative observations are available as in a usual binary classification scenario. In most real world relational datasets this is not the case since they follow a open-world semantics. This means that only positive observations are available. This is the case, for instance, of the Linked Open Data initiative, online social networks and of many recommender systems. Although there has been work done on learning from positive-only observations in different scenarios (Krohn-Grimberghe *et al.*, 2012; Rendle *et al.*, 2009a), learning multi-relational factorization methods from such data is still an open problem.

A summary of models regarding the loss functions they are optimized for, can be found in Table 2.2.

Table 2.2: **Summary of state-of-the-art multi-relational factorization models regarding the loss functions for which they are optimized.**

Method	Loss function	Uses Relation Weights	Target
MRMF	L2	no	single
CMF	Kullback-Leibler Divergence	yes	single
RESCAL-ALS	L2	no	multiple
RESCAL-Logit	Logistic	no	multiple
SME	Energy Matching	no	multiple
MOF-SRP	Logistic	no	multiple
LMF	L2	yes	multiple
MrWTD	L2 and Hinge Loss	yes	multiple

2.2.3 Summary of the presented models

In the previous subsections different aspects of the most prominent multi-factorization models were described. Here a concise summary of them is presented so that is clear which model is meant by which name throughout this thesis.

A complete summary of those models can be found in Table 2.4 which compiles together information from tables 2.1 and 2.2.

2.3 Evaluating Multi-Relational Learning Models

One last question about the multi-relational factorization models is how to evaluate them. Determining the proper evaluation protocol for relational learning models, as for any other machine learning model class, depends on the specific task or application one has in mind. For standard relational regression (where $\mathcal{Y}_r = \mathbb{R}$) or classification tasks ($\mathcal{Y}_r = \{0, 1\}$), standard machine learning evaluation protocols apply. The data D_r about each relation is split into train and test by sampling observations from D_r and putting them to D_r^{test}. The rest of the observations goes to D_r^{train}. The model is then trained on $\{D_r^{\text{train}}\}_{r \in 1,\dots,R}$ and evaluated on $\{D_r^{\text{test}}\}_{r \in 1,\dots,R}$ using a point-wise loss like in Equation 2.1 this is done, for instance by Singh & Gordon (2008b) in the context of rating prediction for recommender systems and in Chapter 5 in the context of semi-supervised binary classification.

However, usually real world datasets represent binary classification problems (i.e. determine the truth value of an observation) but come only with positive observations. A positive-only dataset can be defined as:

$$\{D_r \subseteq \mathcal{X}_r \times \{1\}\}_{r \in 1,\dots,R} \;.$$

This happens because most of the relational knowledge bases follow an open-world assumption, i.e. while observations in the database are assumed to be true, nothing can be said about the truth value of statements not in the dataset. This is, for instance, the case for RDF datasets where observed triples are assumed to be true and unobserved ones have unknown truth value (Drumond *et al.*, 2012). The same happens in social networks. One can say that two users know each other (even if only digitally) if they are connected through a friendship relation. However if they are not connected in the social network they might still know each other in the real world. Another example comes from the recommender systems area. A user may purchase a product from a different store, so the fact that it is not observed in the database that the user bought a specific item does not mean that he/she did not buy it or is not interested in it.

The problem with positive only data is that machine learning models need to be trained on examples of all possible classes, which means that both positive and negative examples are needed. In order to train models for this task, it is necessary to generate negative examples. These are simply assumed to be everything not observed in the database. One commonly used evaluation methodology in the literature is the one employed by Jenatton *et al.* (2012). The negative examples are assumed to be:

$$\{D_{r,-}\}_{r\in 1,\dots,R} := \{(x_1, x_2, 0)|(x_1, x_2, 1) \notin D_r \wedge (x_1, x_2) \in \mathcal{X}_r\} \ .$$

and the available data for one relation is then represented as:

$$D_r^* := D_r \cup D_{r,-} \quad \text{while the whole dataset is given by } D := \{D_r^*\}_{r\in 1,\dots,R}$$

so that the data D can be split into train D^{train} and test D^{test} sets as in a typical binary classification scenario. Since this approach first samples negative examples and then splits the data, we will call it the *Sample and split* protocol. The fallback of this approach when working with positive-only data under the open-world assumption is that, for each negative example $(x_1, x_2, 0) \in D_r^{\text{train}}$ observed during training, the model can be sure that $(x_1, x_2, 1) \notin D_r^{\text{test}}$. This is because this protocol samples negative train examples from

$$\{(x_1, x_2, 0)|(x_1, x_2, 1) \notin D_r^{\text{train}} \cup D_r^{\text{test}} \wedge (x_1, x_2) \in \mathcal{X}_r\}$$

meaning that there is some contamination of the training data with information about the test partition. This happens because, in a real world positive only scenario, one has only access to data points in $\{D_r^{\text{train}}\}_{r\in 1,\dots,R}$. Thus, in order to properly simulate this situation, an evaluation protocol for positive-only data should sample negative train examples $D_{r,-}^{\text{train}}$ from

$$D_{r,-}^{\text{train}} \sim \{(x_1, x_2, 0)|(x_1, x_2, 1) \notin D_r^{\text{train}} \wedge (x_1, x_2) \in \mathcal{X}_r\}$$

and then sample negative test examples $\{D_{r,-}^{\text{test}}\}$ from

$$D_{r,-}^{\text{test}} \sim \{(x_1, x_2, 0)|(x_1, x_2, 1) \notin D_r^{\text{train}} \cup D_r^{\text{test}} \wedge (x_1, x_2) \in \mathcal{X}_r\} \ .$$

Finally the models are evaluated using a pairwise loss like in Equation 2.2. This approach has been widely used to evaluate item prediction models in the area of recommender systems (Cremonesi *et al.*, 2010; Rendle *et al.*, 2009a,b) but, so far, it is not commonly used by the relational factorization community. We will refer to this protocol as the *Split and Sample* approach. This is the approach used in chapters 3 and 4, since they deal with positive only data.

Although subtle, the difference between the two approaches lies in how to generate the negative examples for training models with positive-only data. Table 2.3 summarizes the difference between Sample-and-Split and Split-and-Sample.

Table 2.3: **Comparison between the sampling strategies for tasks where only positive observations are available.**

Strategy	$\{D_{r,-}^{\text{train}}\}_{r \in 1,...,R}$
Sample and Split	$\{(x_1, x_2, 0) \mid (x_1, x_2, 1) \notin D_r^{\text{train}} \cup D_r^{\text{test}} \wedge (x_1, x_2) \in \mathcal{X}_r\}$
Split and Sample	$\{(x_1, x_2, 0) \mid (x_1, x_2, 1) \notin D_r^{\text{train}} \wedge (x_1, x_2) \in \mathcal{X}_r\}$

2.4 Open Problems in Multi-Relational Factorization

From the discussion in the previous section one can summarize some of the most important findings in the area of multi-relational factorization models. First of all, using relation latent features in the model is important when dealing with different relations that involve the same entity types (signature clash problem). Such features might be represented as a vector (or a diagonal matrix) or as a dense matrix. The latter approach is usually favored because it can cope with asymmetric relations. Another important finding is that weighting the contribution of each relation to the overall loss the model is optimized for, leads to models with better predictive performance.

Although a lot of work has been done in the area of Multi-Relational factorization, there are still some open questions not answered by the state-of-the-art. Some of these questions are summarized in the following.

- It is still not clear *how to optimally treat positive only observations*. Most of the work on multi-relational factorization assumes that one has both positive and negative data points at hand. However this is not the case for many real world applications. Chapter 3 of this thesis builds on previous work from the recommender systems literature on learning from positive only instances (Rendle *et al.*, 2009a) and investigates further this issue on RDF datasets.

- One topic not yet fully covered in the related work is how to *properly optimize the factorization model for a number of different target relations.* Existing models focus either on (i) one single target relation or (ii) learn one model which performance is a compromise on the performance on all target relations. Chapter 4 proposes a specific parametrization of the prediction function depending on the target relation. This way, it is possible to find optimal parameters per target relation.

- How to *automatically learn the relation weights*, i.e. the α_r parameters. A first attempt to this problem has been made by Simsekli *et al.* (2013). Their approach is however very specific to their own model. distribution over them so that they can also be sampled from the posterior.

- It is not clear from the state-of-the-art whether modeling pairwise effects like MOF-SRP does have advantages over modeling only three-way interactions like RESCAL. Although Jenatton *et al.* (2012) compared MOF-SRP against RESCAL, both models are optimized for different loss functions, being hard to determine the effect of the pairwise modeling. This is examined in Chapter 3.

Table 2.4: **Complete summary of state-of-the-art models**

Method	Reference	Prediction function $\hat{y}_r(x_1, x_2)$	Relation features	Loss function	Uses Relation Weights	Target
MRMF	(Lippert *et al.*, 2008)	$\varphi(x_1)^\top \varphi(x_2)$	none	L2	no	single
CMF	(Singh & Gordon, 2008b)	$\varphi(x_1)^\top \varphi(x_2)$	none	Kullback-Leibler Divergence	yes	single
SME	(Glorot *et al.*, 2013)	$(\mathbf{W}_s\varphi(x_1)^\top + \mathbf{W}_s\Phi_r^\top + \mathbf{B}_s)^\top + (\mathbf{W}_o\varphi(x_2)^\top + \mathbf{W}_o\Phi_r^\top + \mathbf{B}_o)^\top$	diagonal matrix	Energy Matching	no	multiple
RESCAL	(Nickel *et al.*, 2011)	$\varphi(x_1)^\top \Phi_r \varphi(x_2)$	full matrix	L2	no	multiple
RESCAL-Logit	(Nickel & Tresp, 2013)	$\varphi(x_1)^\top \Phi_r \varphi(x_2)$	full matrix	Logistic	no	multiple
MOF-SRP	(Jenatton *et al.*, 2012)	$\mathbf{a}\Phi_r\mathbf{a}^\top + \varphi(x_1)\Phi_r\mathbf{b}^\top + \mathbf{b}\Phi_r\varphi(x_2)^\top + \varphi(x_1)^\top\Phi_r\varphi(x_2)$	$\Phi_r = \sum_{j=1}^{d} w_j^r \mathbf{u}_j \mathbf{v}_j^\top$	Logistic	no	multiple
LMF	(Agarwal *et al.*, 2011)	$\varphi(x_1)^\top \Phi_{r,0}^\top \Phi_{r,1} \varphi(x_2)$	$\Phi_r = \Phi_{r,0}^\top \Phi_{r,1}$	L2	yes	multiple
MrWTD	(London *et al.*, 2012)	$\gamma(b_r + \varphi(x_1)^\top \Phi_r \varphi(x_2))$	full matrix	L2 and Hinge Loss	yes	multiple

Chapter 3

Loss functions for multi-relational learning tasks

Contents

In Chapter 2 it was stated that, although state-of-the-art multi-relational factorization models have come a long way, there is still no specific study about how to optimally learn from relational data with positive only observations. This problem has been well studied in the context of recommender systems and is closely examined here for multi-relational data, more specifically on mining RDF databases, since they are vastly found on the Internet and its open-world semantics implies that only positive observations are available. Another open question discussed in this chapter is what are the effects of modeling pairwise interactions instead of three-way. The results and findings of this chapter have been published by the author of this thesis in Drumond *et al.* (2012).

The contributions of this chapter are as follows:

1. We approach the problem of triple prediction with multi-relational factorization models and argue that entries corresponding to triples not in the database should be regarded as unobserved entries rather than having value zero.

2. Empirical experiments show that the factorization models can achieve good performance on the task approached here and show that considering the positive-only nature of the data yields better results than dense representations proposed in previous work.

3. From an application point of view an approach is proposed to provide probabilistic estimates of the truth values of RDF triples that are neither explicitly stated in the knowledge base nor can be inferred from logical entailment.

3.1 Application scenario: Mining RDF Knowledge Bases

The Semantic Web and its goal of representing the knowledge contained in Web pages in a machine readable way has generated different standards for this task. RDF is one of such standards and also a W3C recommendation. However, just representing data with RDF is not enough without effective means to access and retrieve this data. Moreover, given the open world semantics of RDF, it is expected that RDF bases are incomplete, thus mining such data for new information is an important task. For instance, many successful approaches for accessing

RDF data have been proposed (Karvounarakis *et al.*, 2003; Prud'hommeaux & Seaborne, 2006; Yang & Kifer, 2003) but they have one limitation in common: they are not able to answer queries when their respective answers are not explicitly encoded in the data nor captured by inference rules. One way to answer such queries is to predict which missing RDF triples related to the query are true given the observed triples. This chapter investigates how to learn multi-relational factorization models from positive-only relational data like RDF databases and propose to go beyond the stored triples and predict new ones given the data, thus being able to answer queries when their answers are not explicit given in the knowledge base. Besides extending the capabilities of existing query mechanisms, such techniques can also be used to aid RDF bases maintainers or support user navigation.

RDF triples are composed by a subject, a predicate and an object. Franz *et al.* (2009) represents this kind of data as a 3-dimensional tensor where one dimension represents the subjects, one the objects and the last one the predicates. Each entry in the tensor has a value 1 for the triples in the database and 0 otherwise. PARAFAC analysis aka Canonical Decomposition (Carroll & Chang, 1970) is then used for deriving authority and hub scores for RDF resources. Here, however, we are interested in predicting the truth value of unobserved triples and hence it is argued that, in contrast to (Franz *et al.*, 2009), one should use a sparse tensor representation, where the positions in the tensor corresponding to triples not in the database are considered to be not observed instead of having a zero value. The task is then to predict the unobserved part of the tensor given the observed one. Methodologically, this scenario is similar (but not equal) to the recommender systems one, where matrix and tensor factorization models have proven to be the best performing models up to this date (Rendle & Schmidt-Thieme, 2010; Rendle *et al.*, 2009b). In this chapter we also investigate the impact of modeling pairwise interactions on relational data and use relational factorization models based on two state-of-the-art tensor factorization models, namely Canonical Decomposition Carroll & Chang (1970) and Pairwise Interaction Tensor Factorization (PITF) (Rendle & Schmidt-Thieme, 2010).

3.1.1 RDF inference and Related Work

There is a vast literature on approaches for querying RDF data. Many of them express RDF data in another formalism such as Frame-Logic (Decker *et al.*, 1998; Yang & Kifer, 2003) and Horn Logic (Sintek *et al.*, 2001) and then exploit the query capabilities of such formalisms. Another set of approaches propose RDF query languages like RQL (Karvounarakis *et al.*, 2003) and SPARQL (Prud'hommeaux & Seaborne, 2006) and propose ways to evaluate queries in such languages as in (Oren *et al.*, 2008). Elbassuoni et al (Elbassuoni *et al.*, 2009) proposed to augment RDF queries with keywords and use statistical information retrieval models to rank query results. Although these are relevant and successful ideas, they have one limitation in common: they do not exploit facts that are not explicitly encoded in the data and cannot be captured by inference rules. The approach proposed here relies on machine learning techniques to predict the truth value of such RDF triples. Work has been done on introducing uncertainty in RDF by attaching probabilities to triples (Udrea *et al.*, 2006) and on how to query such probabilistic RDF databases (Huang & Liu, 2009). The task considered in this chapter, however, is to discover new information in traditional RDF bases.

Tensor Factorization models have been studied and applied for many years in many different fields. One prominent and general approach is Tucker decomposition (Tucker, 1966). A special case of Tucker decomposition (TD) is the Canonical Decomposition (CD) (Carroll & Chang, 1970). A special case of CD, the Pairwise Interaction Tensor Factorization (PITF) model has been proposed by Rendle & Schmidt-Thieme (2010), which explicitly models pairwise interactions between entities in the data. In Franz *et al.* (2009), a tensor based representation of RDF data is proposed. They have shown that making predictions over RDF triples can be cast as a tensor factorization task. In their work they used CD to derive authority and hub scores for RDF resources in order to rank them. Here instead, we are interested in predicting the truth values of triples that do not appear in the dataset. The RESCAL model from Nickel *et al.* (2011) is also a tensor factorization model for relational data. Both Nickel *et al.* (2011) and Franz *et al.* (2009) implicitly assume that triples not appearing in the dataset are false. In the context of this work, the truth values of triples which are not in the dataset are considered to be unobserved and the goal of the models proposed here is to predict which triples are most likely to be true. Here the factorization models are optimized for the Bayesian Personalized Ranking (BPR) criterion (as in Rendle & Schmidt-Thieme (2010)) and it is analyzed how explicitly modeling pairwise interactions capture the interactions among subjects, predicates and objects of RDF triples.

3.2 Predicting RDF Triples

According to the W3C RDF specification (Klyne & Carroll, 2004), an RDF dataset is a set of statements, each one of them consisting of a subject, a predicate and an object. Let S be the set of all subjects, P the set of all predicates and O the set of all objects. An RDF dataset is denoted by $T \subseteq S \times P \times O$. From this one can clearly see that an RDF database is a relational dataset. In the terminology introduced in Chapter 2, the properties are the relations while the subjects and the objects are the entities, such that $|P| = R$ and $S \cup O = \mathcal{E}$. The data regarding a given predicate p is given by $D_p \subseteq \mathcal{X}_p \times \mathcal{Y}_p$ such that

$$\mathcal{X}_p \subseteq S \times O$$

and, although $\mathcal{Y}_p := \{0, 1\}$, since only positive observations are available, the data actually is given by $D_p \subseteq \mathcal{X}_p \times \{1\}$.

Also, some ontological information can be encoded in the dataset through RDF Schema (RDFS) (Brickley & Guha, 2004). RDFS is a basic knowledge representation language intended to structure RDF resources. Through RDFS one can define a class hierarchy, and entity type information, which means that for a relation p, a given observation (x_1, x_2) can be true, i.e. $(x_1, x_2, 1) \in D_p$ iff the subject x_1 belongs to the domain of the predicate p, i.e. $x_1 \in \mathcal{E}_p^{(1)}$ and the object x_2 belongs to the range of p, i.e. $x_2 \in \mathcal{E}_p^{(2)}$.

Before defining the task of RDF triple prediction, we define the concept of a query $(x_1)_p$ as a subject-predicate pair. The RDF triple prediction task is to generate a list of objects that, together with a given query, constitute a true observation. More formally, given a query $(x_1)_p$, generate a list of objects x_2 such that $(x_1, x_2, 1) \in D_p$. One approach to this problem would be to generate a list with all the objects that meet the range restriction of the predicate in the query. However, in real world datasets, some (or most) of the information about properties ranges and domains and class membership may be missing. Furthermore, not all objects will form a true triple with the given pair. Thus it makes sense to deliver a list of objects ranked according to the likelihood that $(x_1, x_2, 1) \in D_p$. If some information about the range of the predicate in the pair is available, the objects $x_2 \notin \mathcal{E}_p^{(2)}$ can be excluded from the ranked list. Therefore this can be formulated as a ranking problem, the objective function being the one depicted in equation 2.2.

3.3 Predicting RDF triples by Tensor Factorization

As already shown by Franz *et al.* (2009), RDF data can be represented as a tensor where the triples in T are the positive observations. Tensor factorization models approximate the original tensor by a set of low-rank matrices and differ in the number of such matrices and in the way they are combined to reconstruct the tensor. The low-rank matrices used are the ones that are optimal according to some loss function (e.g. the reconstruction error or some other optimization criterion suited for the task at hand). In the following we discuss the optimization criterion and the factorization models applied for predicting RDF triples.

3.3.1 Factorization Models

Next, we show how factorization can model the latent dependencies in RDF graphs. We discuss the Canonical decomposition (CD) or PARAFAC analysis, which has already been applied for analyzing Semantic Web data (Franz *et al.*, 2009), as well as the more recent Pairwise Interaction Tensor Factorization (PITF) model (Rendle & Schmidt-Thieme, 2010). We investigate also what the underlying assumption of each model means for representing RDF triples.

3.3.1.1 Three-way Interaction Model

The three way interaction model learns three latent feature mappings, namely one for the subjects $\varphi^S : S \to \mathbb{R}^k$, one for the objects $\varphi^O : O \to \mathbb{R}^k$ and one set of features for each predicate $\Phi_p \in \mathbb{R}^{k \times k}$. If one assumes that the relation feature matrices are diagonal matrices, this model is equivalent to the Canonical Decomposition of a tensor and thus will be referred to as CD model. The prediction function is given by Equation 3.1

$$\hat{y}_r^{\text{CD}}(x_1, x_2) := \varphi^S(x_1)^\top \Phi_r \varphi^O(x_2) \tag{3.1}$$

In Franz *et al.* (2009) the CD model is used for analyzing Semantic Web data. Since their aim was to derive authority and hub scores for RDF resources, their approach is not suitable for triple prediction, as shown in Section 3.4, since it lacks an appropriate optimization criterion. Another shortcoming of this approach when predicting RDF triples (as observed in the experiments in Section 3.4) is that it considers that the whole tensor is observed (i.e. triples not on the data are considered to be zeros on the tensor). Thus we call it CD-Dense.

A more appropriate optimization is to use the ranking interpretation (see section 3.2) which leads to pairwise logistic regression (see section 3.3.3 and Rendle *et al.* (2009a)). Also, due to open world assumption, it makes sense to consider that only one portion of the tensor is observed (i.e. triples that are not in the dataset are considered as unobserved data) thus making use of a sparse representation of the tensor. We will follow Rendle *et al.* (2009a) and refer to the pairwise ranking optimization as the Bayesian Personalized Ranking (BPR) – i.e. a CD model optimized for BPR is called CD-BPR.

3.3.1.2 Pairwise Interaction Model

One problem with CD is that it considers only the three-wise interaction among subjects, predicates and objects. In the problem definition, however, it was stated that properties are related to subjects through their domain and to objects through their range. Interactions between subjects and objects are also relevant. For instance, musicians are more likely to be related to songs, bands and musical instruments than to birds, or touristic destinations. Thus it makes sense to use a factorization model that explicitly takes into account those pairwise interactions.

The pairwise interaction model is equivalent to the PITF decomposition of a tensor and learns six feature mappings, namely two mappings for the subjects, being one for subject-object interaction, $\varphi_O^S : S \to \mathbb{R}^k$ and another one for the subject-relation interaction $\varphi_P^S : S \to \mathbb{R}^k$; two for the objects being one for the subject-object interaction $\varphi_S^O : O \to \mathbb{R}^k$ and one for the object-relation interaction $\varphi_P^O : O \to \mathbb{R}^k$; and two feature vectors for each relation $p \in 1, \ldots, R$ namely $\Phi_p^S \in \mathbb{R}^k$ and $\Phi_p^O \in \mathbb{R}^k$.

This way, PITF explicitly models the two-way interactions between subjects, predicates and objects by factorizing each of the three relationships:

$$\hat{y}_r^{\text{PITF}}(x_1, x_2) = \varphi_O^S(x_1)^\top \varphi_S^O(x_2) + \varphi_P^O(x_2)^\top \Phi_r^O + \varphi_P^S(x_1)^\top \Phi_r^S \qquad (3.2)$$

It is important to state that the subject-predicate interaction vanishes for predicting rankings of objects for a given *(subject, predicate)* pair. Indeed, when computing the rank of an object x_2 for a given pair (x_1, p), the subject and the predicate of the triple are known in advance. Therefore we want to predict only the object, thus being interested only in the interactions between x_1 and x_2 and between p and x_2. This way the mappings φ_P^S and Φ^S are no longer needed.

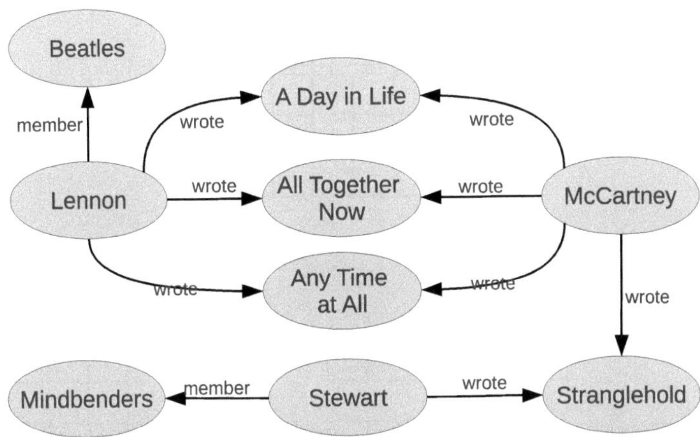

Figure 3.1: Example of a small RDF graph

Thus, the final model parameters are $\varphi^S : S \to \mathbb{R}^k$, $\Phi \in \mathbb{R}^{|P| \times k}$, $\varphi_S^O : O \to \mathbb{R}^k$, and $\varphi_P^O : O \to \mathbb{R}^k$ and the final model equation for PITF is:

$$\hat{y}_r^{\mathrm{PITF}}(x_1, x_2) = \varphi^S(x_1)^\top \varphi_S^O(x_2) + \Phi_r^\top \cdot \varphi_P^O(x_2) \tag{3.3}$$

As shown in Rendle & Schmidt-Thieme (2010), this is exactly what happens when optimizing PITF for the BPR-Opt) criterion (see Section 3.3.3).

3.3.2 The open world assumption and the loss function

In order to unserstand what the open world assumption is about, let us have a look on a small example of an RDF dataset depicted as a graph in Figure 3.1. There, the predicates are represented by the edges while the subjects and objects are the nodes.

As already shown by Franz *et al.* (2009), RDF data can be represented as a tensor where the triples in T are the positive observations. For instance, the graph from Figure 3.1 can be represented as the tensor in Figure 3.2. The names of the graph nodes from Figure 3.1 are abbreviated on Figure 3.2 (e.g. *A Day in Life* is *ADL* in Figure 3.2). The observations in the data are denoted with a "+" sign. The task is to predict which of the empty positions in the tensor should be filled with a "+". This means that the missing triples are unobserved data

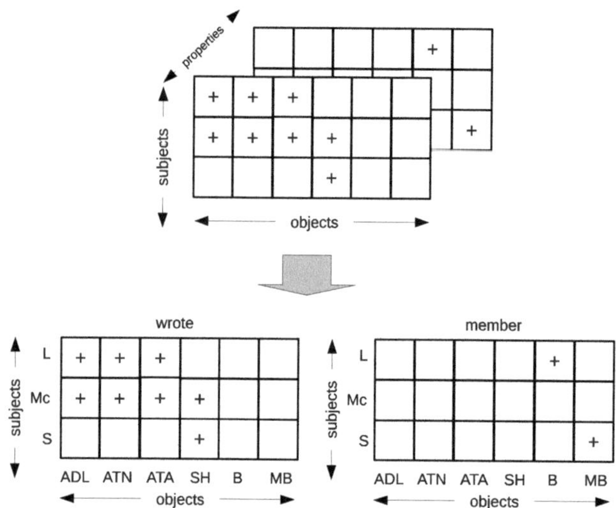

Figure 3.2: RDF graph from Figure 3.1 represented as a tensor. On the bottom, the slices of the tensor are placed next to each other.

rather than negative examples. One reason for this is that, according to the RDF specification Klyne & Carroll (2004), open world semantics is assumed, i.e. the truth values of triples that are not in the dataset are considered to be unobserved instead of being false.

However, when optimizing the models for a pointwise loss like the squared error, one needs both positive and negative examples. In the case of the squared loss, the target space is assumed to be $\mathcal{Y}_p = \{0, 1\}$, where $y_p = 1$ for positive observation and $y_p = 0$ for negative ones and the loss looks like:

$$L(D, \hat{y}) := \sum_{p \in R} \sum_{(x_1, x_2, y_p) \in D_p} (y - \hat{y}_p(x_1, x_2))^2$$

Dealing with the open world assumption has much to do with the fact that only positive observations are available, i.e. observations of the kind $(x_1, x_2, 1)$. Be $(x_1, x_2, 1) \in D_p^{train}$ the train data for relation p, the set of negative examples are considered to be all observations

$$D_{p,-} := \{(x_1, x_2, 0) | (x_1, x_2, 1) \notin D_p^{\text{train}} \wedge (x_1, x_2) \in \mathcal{X}_p\}$$

This is equivalent to filling the unobserved entries in the tensor from Figure 3.2 with "-" signs. The approach from Franz *et al.* (2009) optimizes a CD model for an unregularized squared loss such that the data for a given relation p is $D_p := D_p^{\text{train}} \cup D_{p,-}$. Since, in the tensor interpretation of the RDF data this is equivalent to filling the missing entries with 0, we call it a *dense* approach. This approach has two main drawbacks. First, it does not scale well for tensors of moderate sizes given the number of negative examples inserted. Second, since it is unregularized, the model simply overfits the data and learns that all examples which are not positive in the training data should be negative, which clearly violates the open world assumption. RESCAL, however has a more principled machine learning approach to the problem. By regularizing the model with the Tikhonov regularization, it prevents it from overfitting the data. A strategy to solve the scalability issue, is proposed by Jenatton *et al.* (2012), in which only a subset of the negative examples $D_{p,-}^{train} \subset D_{p,-}$ are sampled.

3.3.3 Dealing with the open world assumption through the BPR Framework

One crucial difference between the approaches from Franz *et al.* (2009) and Nickel *et al.* (2011) and the one proposed here is that we explicitly consider the positive-only scenario (see Section 2.3) when training the model. The reason behind this is that that, according to the RDF specification (Klyne & Carroll, 2004), open world semantics is assumed, i.e. the truth values of triples that are not in the dataset are considered to be unobserved instead of being false. Thus RDF datasets consist only of positive observations.

Since there are no negative examples in the dataset we use the *Split and Sample* approach to generate negative training examples. Like in Rendle & Schmidt-Thieme (2010), we assume that, given a query $(x_1)_p$, an object x_2 is more relevant than another object x_2' iff it is true that $(x_1, x_2, 1) \in D_p^{train}$ and $(x_1, x_2', 1) \notin D_p^{train}$. This can be seen as a ranking constraint, i.e. the object x_2 should be ranked higher than the object x_2'.

In Section 3.2, the triple prediction problem was formulated as a ranking problem. Thus, in order to obtain good results on this task, one should use parameters that are optimal according to a ranking criterion. Thus, both PITF and the sparse version of CD are optimized here for the Bayesian Personalized Ranking optimization criterion (BPR-Opt) (Rendle *et al.*, 2009a), shown in equation

3.4. In order to get better rankings, BPR-Opt) should be maximized, i.e. one should search for the model parameters that deliver its highest value.

$$\text{BPR-Opt} := \sum_{p} \sum_{(x_1,x_2,1)\in D_p^{\text{train}}} \sum_{(x_1,x_2',0)\in D_{p,-}^{\text{train}}} \ln \sigma(\hat{y}_p(x_1, x_2) - \hat{y}_p(x_1, x_2')) - \lambda_\Theta ||\Theta||_F^2$$

$$(3.4)$$

In equation 3.4, σ is the logistic function $\sigma(x) := \frac{1}{1+e^{-x}}$, Θ are the model parameters, λ_Θ is the regularization constant and $|| \cdot ||_F$ is the Frobenius norm. It can be easily seen that the BPR loss is an instance of the pairwise loss in Equation 2.2. In the experiments performed here, the latent factor matrices of both CD-BPR and PITF are the ones that maximize BPR-Opt) in the training data. They are learned using a stochastic gradient descent algorithm depicted in Algorithm 1 for CD-BPR and in Algorithm 2. For the complete derivation of this optimization criterion and the learning algorithm for optimizing the parameters for BPR-Opt), the reader is referred to Rendle & Schmidt-Thieme (2010); Rendle *et al.* (2009a).

3.3.4 Filtering the Results of Tensor Factorization Models

In order to improve the performance of the approach proposed here, we propose to filter out unreasonable results using range and class membership information. The filter works as follows. Given a pair (x_1, p), a tensor factorization model can derive a total order over the objects in $\mathcal{E}$. The filter takes this order and returns an ordered list containing only the objects that belong to the range of predicate p, i.e. $x_2 \in \mathcal{E}_p^{(2)}$. This is done by changing the scoring function of the models as follows:

$$\hat{y}_p'(x_1, x_2) = \begin{cases} -\infty & \text{if } x_2 \notin \mathcal{E}_p^{(2)} \\ \hat{y}_p(x_1, x_2) & \text{otherwise.} \end{cases}$$

$$(3.5)$$

where $\hat{y}_p(x_1, x_2)$ is the scoring function of the unfiltered model. As a side note, it should be pointed that this is just a formalization. In an actual implementation it is enough to rank only elements $x \in \mathcal{E}_p^{(2)}$.

If no information about $\mathcal{E}_p^{(2)}$ is given, the results remain as they are, i.e. $\hat{y}_p'(x_1, x_2) = \hat{y}_p(x_1, x_2)$.

Algorithm 1 **CD-BPR**

1: **procedure** LEARNCD-BPR

  input: number of relations R, training data $\{D_r\}_{r=1,\dots,R}$, set of subjects S
  and objects O, learning rate η, and regularization constant λ

  output: latent features $(\varphi^S, \varphi^O, \Phi)$

2:    $\forall_{x \in S}\ \varphi^S(x) \sim \mathcal{N}(0, \sigma^2 \mathbf{I})$

3:    $\forall_{x \in O}\ \varphi^O(x) \sim \mathcal{N}(0, \sigma^2 \mathbf{I})$

4:    **for** $r = 1, \dots, R$ **do**

5:        $\Phi_r \sim \mathcal{N}(0, \sigma^2 \mathbf{I})$

6:    **end for**

7:    **repeat**

8:        $r \sim \mathrm{Uniform}(1, R)$

9:        $(x_1, x_2, 1) \sim \mathrm{Uniform}(D_r^{\mathrm{train}})$

10:        $x_2' \sim \mathrm{Uniform}(\{x | (x_1, x, 0) \in D_{r,-}^{\mathrm{train}}\})$

11:        $\delta \leftarrow (1 - \sigma(\hat{y}_p(x_1, x_2) - \hat{y}_p(x_1, x_2')))$

12:        $\varphi^S(x_1) \leftarrow \varphi^S(x_1) + \eta(\delta \cdot \Phi_r^\top (\varphi^O(x_2) - \varphi^O(x_2')) - \lambda \varphi^S(x_1))$

13:        $\varphi^O(x_2) \leftarrow \varphi^O(x_2) + \eta(\delta \cdot \varphi^S(x_1)^\top \Phi_r - \lambda \varphi^O(x_2))$

14:        $\varphi^O(x_2') \leftarrow \varphi^O(x_2') + \eta(-\delta \cdot \varphi^S(x_1)^\top \Phi_r - \lambda \varphi^O(x_2'))$

15:        $\Phi_r \leftarrow \Phi_r + \eta(\delta \cdot \varphi^S(x_1)(\varphi^O(x_2) - \varphi^O(x_2')) - \lambda \Phi_r)$

16:    **until** convergence

17:    **return** $(\varphi^S, \varphi^O, \Phi)$

18: **end procedure**

Algorithm 2 PITF-BPR

1: **procedure** LEARNPITF-BPR
    input: number of relations R, training data $\{D_r\}_{r=1,\dots,R}$, set of subjects S
    and objects O, learning rate η, and regularization constant λ
    output: latent features $(\varphi^S, \varphi_S^O, \varphi_P^O, \Phi)$

2:    $\forall_{x \in S}\ \varphi^S(x) \sim \mathcal{N}(0, \sigma^2 \mathbf{I})$
3:    $\forall_{x \in O}\ \varphi_S^O(x) \sim \mathcal{N}(0, \sigma^2 \mathbf{I})$
4:    $\forall_{x \in O}\ \varphi_P^O(x) \sim \mathcal{N}(0, \sigma^2 \mathbf{I})$
5:    **for** $r = 1, \dots, R$ **do**
6:        $\Phi_r \sim \mathcal{N}(0, \sigma^2 \mathbf{I})$
7:    **end for**
8:    **repeat**
9:        $r \sim \text{Uniform}(1, R)$
10:      $(x_1, x_2, 1) \sim \text{Uniform}(D_r^{\text{train}})$
11:      $x_2' \sim \text{Uniform}(\{x | (x_1, x, 0) \in D_{r,-}^{\text{train}}\})$
12:      $\delta \leftarrow (1 - \sigma(\hat{y}_p(x_1, x_2) - \hat{y}_p(x_1, x_2')))$
13:      $\varphi^S(x_1) \leftarrow \varphi^S(x_1) + \eta(\delta \cdot (\varphi_S^O(x_2) - \varphi_S^O(x_2')) - \lambda \varphi^S(x_1))$
14:      $\varphi_S^O(x_2) \leftarrow \varphi_S^O(x_2) + \eta(\delta \cdot \varphi^S(x_1) - \lambda \varphi_S^O(x_2))$
15:      $\varphi_S^O(x_2') \leftarrow \varphi_S^O(x_2') + \eta(-\delta \cdot \varphi^S(x_1) - \lambda \varphi_S^O(x_2'))$
16:      $\varphi_P^O(x_2) \leftarrow \varphi_P^O(x_2) + \eta(\delta \cdot \Phi_r - \lambda \varphi_P^O(x_2))$
17:      $\varphi_P^O(x_2') \leftarrow \varphi_P^O(x_2') + \eta(-\delta \cdot \Phi_r - \lambda \varphi_P^O(x_2'))$
18:      $\Phi_r \leftarrow \Phi_r + \eta(\delta \cdot (\varphi_P^O(x_2) - \varphi_P^O(x_2')) - \lambda \Phi_r)$
19:    **until** convergence
20:    **return** $(\varphi^S, \varphi_S^O, \varphi_P^O, \Phi)$
21: **end procedure**

3.4 Evaluation

In our evaluation, we study the prediction quality of the discussed approaches for the problem of predicting RDF triples. We investigate empirically whether there is an advantage of modeling pairwise interaction on factorization models alone are able to provide reasonable predictions and whether taking the open world assumption into account translates in better results. Then, we evaluate the impact the of proposed filter on the overall performance of the best factorization models.

3.4.1 Datasets

We used four datasets for evaluation:

- *Beatles2* - the same dataset as used in Franz *et al.* (2009). It was extracted from dbpedia.org by crawling other resources starting from *The Beatles*. The dataset is available for download[1];

- *James* - the same as used in Franz *et al.* (2009). It was extracted from db-pedia.org by crawling other resources starting from *James Bond*. The*James* dataset is available for download[2];

- *Properties* - triples containing the properties of the Infobox Ontology[3] extracted from DBpedia version 3.5. It can be downloaded at the DBpedia website[4];

- *SWChallenge* - contains the first 1 million triples of the dataset used in the ISWC Billion Triples Challenge 2009[5].

For the *Properties* and *SWChallenge* datasets we removed the triples with subjects appearing on less than 50 triples. For the *Beatles2* and *James* datasets, this threshold was set to 10, since these datasets are smaller. The characteristics of the preprocessed datasets can be found in table 3.1.

---

[1]http://isweb.uni-koblenz.de/Research/DataSets
[2]http://isweb.uni-koblenz.de/Research/DataSets
[3]http://wiki.dbpedia.org/Ontology
[4]http://wiki.dbpedia.org/Downloads35?v=pb8
[5]http://challenge.semanticweb.org/

Table 3.1: **Dataset characteristics in terms of subjects, predicates, objects, triples and queries**

dataset	Subjects $|S|$	Predicates $|P|$	Objects $|O|$	Triples $\sum_p^R |D_p|$
Beatles2	158	279	5771	11728
James	21	112	851	1335
Properties	200	194	9524	11363
SWChallenge	1010	130	31180	43753

3.4.2 Methods

In this evaluation we want to evaluate the BPR optimized methods discussed in Section 3.3:

- **CD-BPR** - sparse Canonical decomposition optimized for BPR;

- **PITF-BPR** - PITF model optimized for BPR.

So these methods will be compared against the following baselines:

- Most Frequent - suggest the objects that appear in the highest number of triples on the training data;

- Most Frequent per Predicate - for a given pair (s, p), this model suggests the objects that co-occur most frequently with the predicate p on the training data;

- CD-Dense - Canonical decomposition on a dense tensor, i.e. triples that are not on the dataset are considered to be false. This is an application of the method in Franz *et al.* (2009) to the task of triple prediction. We used the same approach for factorizing the tensor as in Franz *et al.* (2009) but we used the scoring function from equation 3.1 instead. As in Franz *et al.* (2009), this model is not regularized.

- RESCAL - the RESCAL model as presented by Nickel *et al.* (2011). This model uses a full matrix as relation features and is optimized for an L2-regularized squared loss (see Table 2.4 for details).

3.4.3 Evaluation Methodology

We split the data into training and test set as follows: for each subject, one predicate is randomly chosen and all the triples containing the subject-predicate pair are put into the test set. The other triples containing the chosen subject are put into the training set. What we want to verify with this evaluation protocol is whether the proposed method is able to predict correctly the triples that were hidden from it (i.e. the ones on the test set).

Once the split was generated, the models were trained on the training set and the prediction quality on the test set was measured. This way we can evaluate if the models are able to answer the queries in the test set by predicting the triples that were actually asserted by the developer of the RDF dataset (i.e. the triples in the test set). The evaluation measures used here were the Precision and Recall in TopN-lists. In order to understand the precision and recall first let us define S_p^{Test} as the set of instances appearing as subjects of a predicate p in the test data:

$$S_p^{\text{Test}} := \{x_1 | \exists_{x_2}(x_1, x_2, 1) \in D_p^{\text{Test}}\}$$

and $O_p^{\text{Test}}(x_1)$ as the instances being related with x_1 by the predicate p as objects:

$$O_p^{\text{Test}}(x_1) := \{x_2 | (x_1, x_2, 1) \in D_p^{\text{Test}}\}$$

The precision and recall for a given relation can be written given as in equations 3.6 and 3.7.

$$\text{Prec}(p, N) := \frac{1}{|S_p^{\text{Test}}|} \sum_{x_1 \in S_p^{\text{Test}}} \frac{|Top(N, x_1, \hat{y}_p, \mathcal{E}) \cap O_p^{\text{Test}}(x_1)|}{N} \tag{3.6}$$

$$\text{Rec}(p, N) := \frac{1}{|S_p^{\text{Test}}|} \sum_{x_1 \in S_p^{\text{Test}}} \frac{|Top(N, x_1, \hat{y}_p, \mathcal{E}) \cap O_p^{\text{Test}}(x_1)|}{|O_p^{\text{Test}}(x_1)|} \tag{3.7}$$

Where $Top(N, x_1, \hat{y}_p, \mathcal{E})$ stands for the N instances x_2 with the highest scores $\hat{y}_p(x_1, x_2)$. The final precision and recall scores are then averaged over all relations as in equations 3.8 and 3.9.

$$\text{Prec}(N) := \frac{1}{|P|} \sum_{p \in P} \text{Prec}(p, N) \tag{3.8}$$

$$\text{Rec}(N) := \frac{1}{|P|} \sum_{p \in P} \text{Rec}(p, N) \tag{3.9}$$

Each experiment was repeated 10 times by sampling new train and test sets and applying the algorithms to them. The results reported here are the averages over the 10 runs.

The CD-BPR and PITF models were learned using the LEARNBPR algorithm (Rendle & Schmidt-Thieme, 2010) and CD-Dense was trained using the alternating least squares algorithm implementation from the MATLAB tensor toolbox[1] (Bader & Kolda, 2006). The hyperparameters were searched on the *Beatles2* dataset using 5-fold cross validation. According to these results, the learn rate was set to 0.05 and the regularization constant to 0.001 for both PITF and CD-BPR. The number of dimensions used was 64 for PITF and for RESCAL, 45 for CD-BPR and 32 for CD-Dense. PITF ran for 500 iterations, while CD-BPR for 1000. We observed that, for CD-Dense, using higher dimensions leads to a deterioration of the prediction quality, since the model assumes that unobserved triples have value 0 on the tensor. This way, the prediction for all the test triples also gets closer to 0.

3.4.4 Results

Figure 3.3 shows the Precision-Recall curves on all datasets for TopN-lists varying from 1 to 10^2. There one can see that PITF achieves a higher prediction quality on all datasets. For both the smaller and larger datasets PITF outperformed CD-BPR and the other baselines. This result constitutes an evidence that the subject-object and predicate-object pairwise interactions captured by PITF do play an important role when determining new triples. The results also show that the CD-Dense is not appropriate for this task. One reason for this is the implicit assumption that triples not on the dataset are false. The values for such triples on the tensor are set to zero and the learned model tends to predict low scores for any triple that was not on the training data. Please note that in Franz *et al.* (2009), this approach was developed for a different task. The results here show that using a dense tensor representation is not suitable for our scenario.

---

[1]Please note that this toolbox has also been used by Franz *et al.* (2009) for deriving authorities and hub scores for RDF resources.

[2]The results published in Drumond *et al.* (2012) did not contain RESCAL as a baseline. These results were computed for this thesis, thus after the paper has been published.

One last point worth mentioning is the good performance of RESCAL, although it is optimized for the squared loss. This is an evidence, as discussed in Chapter 2 that using a full matrix leads to better predictive accuracy. However it is still outperformed by PITF-BPR indicating the benefits of optimizing for the BPR-Opt) loss. To clear measure this benefit, one needs to check how the exact same model performs when optimized both for the regularized squared loss and for BPR-Opt), as seen on Figure 3.4 for PITF and Figure 3.5 for CD. These results are discussed in the next subsection.

To illustrate the usefulness of the models proposed here, we trained the PITF model on the whole *Beatles2* dataset (i.e. without splitting it into training and test set) and computed the rankings for 4 different queries that were not on the dataset. Such queries are:

- *What is the musical style of the song Little Child?* - possible correct answers would be *Rock_and_roll* and *Rock_music*. In the Last.fm website[1] the most popular tags for the *Little child* resource are *classic rock* and *rock*. This query is represented by *(Little_Child, musicalStyle)*.

- *The song All I've Got To Do is from which album?* - this song is part of the track list of the album *With the Beatles*, which was the second studio album by the Beatles and was released in 1963. The query is represented by *(All_Ive_Got_to_Do, fromAlbum)*.

- *The song Savoy Truffle is from which band?* - represented by *(Savoy_Truffle, band)*. *Savoy Truffle* is a song by the Beatles.

- *Who was/were the writer(s) of the Help! album?* - represented by *(Help_album, writer)*. The *Help album* is an album which songs were written by the Beatles, but most of them by John Lennon and Paul McCartney.

Table 3.2 shows the 5 best ranked objects for each query. Note that, for all queries, the correct answers appear among the 5 best ranked ones. For the *(Help_album, writer)* query, the object *Beatles_for_Sale* was ranked with the highest score although it does not interact with the predicate *writer*. However, it interacts with the subject *Help_album* through predicates like *wikilink* and *lastAlbum*.

---

[1]http://www.last.fm

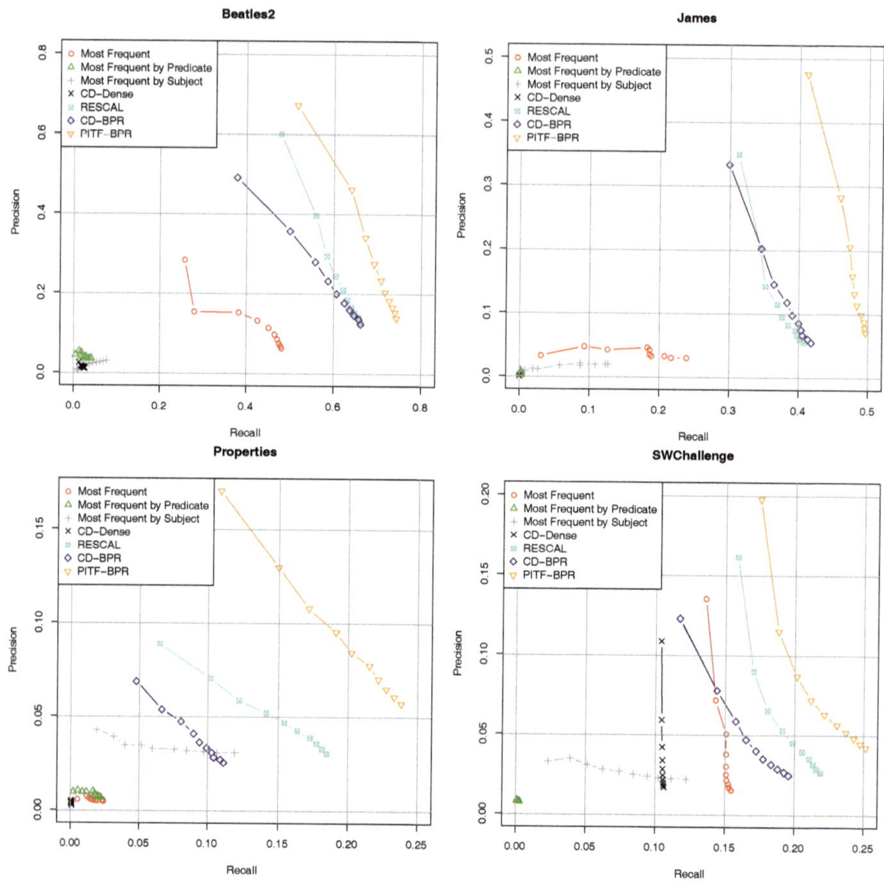

Figure 3.3: Precision-Recall Curves for the RDF datasets

3.4.5 Comparing BPR against RMSE

One question that remains open is how big is the impact of the optimization for
BPR-Opt) alone. In order to examinate this we optimized both PITF and CD for
the L2-regularized squared loss, called PITF-RMSE and CD-RMSE, respectively
and compared them against their BPR optimized variants.

Table 3.2: **Top-5 lists generated by the PITF model for 4 different queries. The PITF model was trained on the whole *Beatles2* dataset. Namespaces were omitted to improve readability**

(Little_Child, musicalStyle)		*(All_Ive_Got_to_Do, fromAlbum)*	
Object	**Score**	**Object**	**Score**
Rock_and_roll	9.24064	With_the_Beatles	8.66325
Rock_music	9.11723	The_Beatles_Second_Album	7.20028
Beat_music	7.43717	1963	6.11425
With_the_Beatles	6.69691	11_September	6.04095
Pop_music	6.65818	Beatles_for_Sale	6.01018
(Savoy_Truffle, band)		*(Help_album, writer)*	
Object	**Score**	**Object**	**Score**
The_Beatles	9.14638	Beatles_for_Sale	7.39417
Rocky_Raccoon	7.43487	The_Beatles	7.25562
Yer_Blues	7.29677	Lennon/McCartney	7.10224
Im_So_Tired	7.26367	Rubber_Soul	6.99047
Wild_Honey_Pie	7.18472	I_Need_You_The_Beatles_song	6.98841

Figure 3.4 shows the comparison for the PITF model. There one can clearly see that optimizing the same model with the BPR framework leads to better results than optimizing it for a regularized squared loss. One interesting fact is that the improvements are higher for the top positions then for the bottom positions.

The same can be observed for the CD model in Figure 3.5. While the unregularized CD-Dense proved not to work for predictive tasks (as seen on Figure 3.3), the regularized CD-RMSE is able to provide reasonable results, which are further improved by optimizing the model for BPR-Opt). Here the fact that the benefits of the BPR optimization are more pronounced for the higher positions of the list is even more noticeable than for the PITF figure.

3.4.6 Evaluation of Type information through Post Filter

When answering a query all objects are given a score. Thus it may sometimes happen that some unreasonable answer to a query is highly ranked. One example of this can be seen in Table 3.2 where the object *Beatles_for_Sale* was the best ranked for the *(Help_album, writer)* query. Most of such unreasonable answers

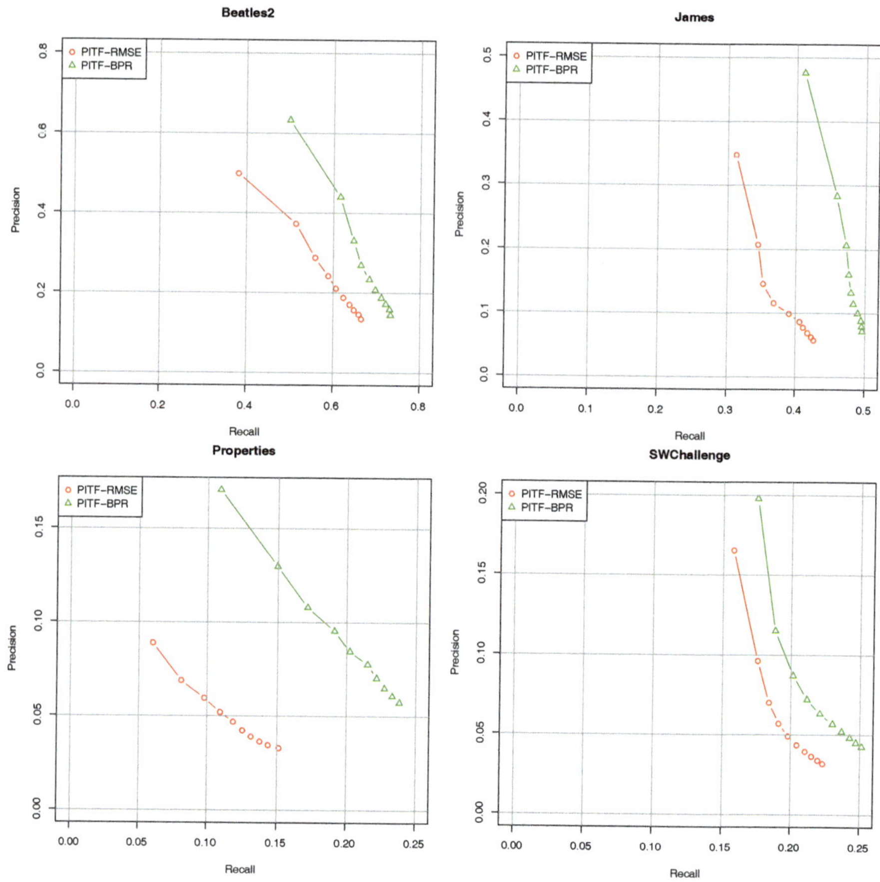

Figure 3.4: Comparison between PITF-BPR and PITF-RMSE

can be detected through simple entity type checking as done by the post filter in Section 3.3.4.

Figure 3.6 helps to understand why this happens. In order to generate this figure, the PITF model was trained on the *Beatles2* dataset with the same parameters as before, but only with 2 latent dimensions. This way, each object x_2 is represented by two latent factor vectors, namely $(\varphi_S^O(x_2)_1, \varphi_S^O(x_2)_2)$ and

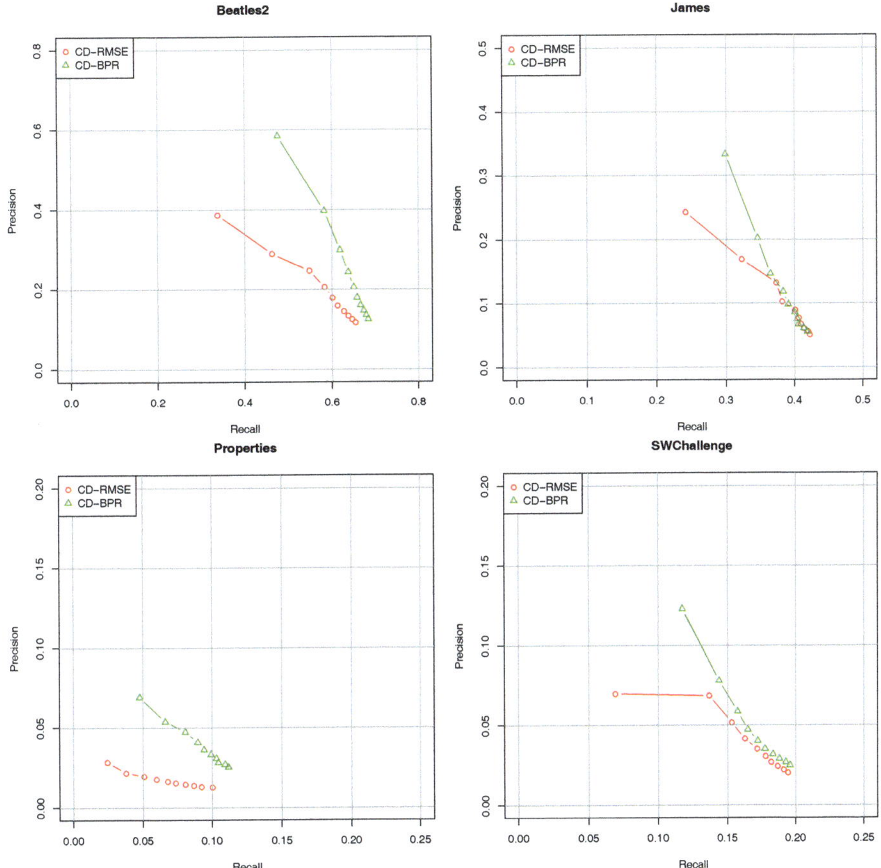

Figure 3.5: Comparison between CD-BPR and CD-RMSE

$(\varphi_P^O(x_2)_1, \varphi_P^O(x_2)_2)$. In Figure 3.6 one can see the plot of each vector $\varphi_P^O(x_2)$ as a point in $\mathbb{R}^2$. We distinguish four kinds of objects: **classes** like *"Person"*, *"Song"* and *"Country"*; **individuals** like *"Eric Clapton"*, *"While my Guitar Gently Weeps"* and *"England"*; **textual descriptions** of the objects; and **other** kinds of resources like dates and other instances of primitive data types such as integer numbers. In Figure 3.6 is possible to see that, only with two latent factors,

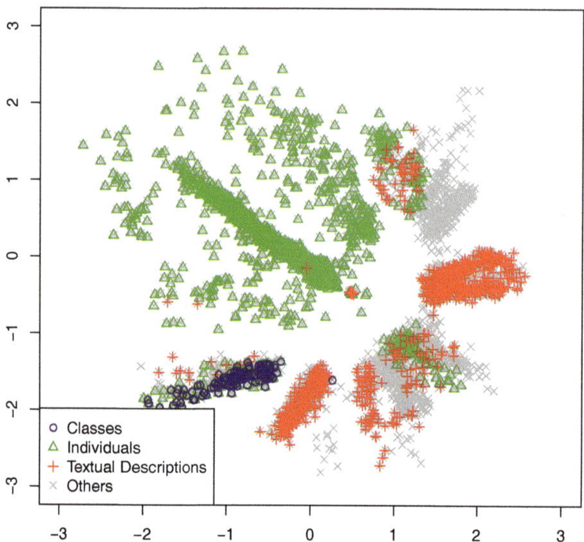

Figure 3.6: Plots of object latent factors by PITF with 2 dimensions. Note how objects of the same type are grouped together in the same region of the space.

PITF is already able to group together instances of different types. There are however still some regions where objects of different types are grouped together and objects from this area are, most likely, the ones that appear as "unreasonable" answers.

Still the following question remains: how big is the impact of filtering based on type information on the performance of the models? Figure 3.7 shows the results of applying the filter the output of PITF-BPR and CD-BPR methods on the *Beatles2* dataset. The first conclusion drawn from the experiments is that the performance improvement is not significant. The main reason for this is that on this dataset most of the information about predicate ranges and class membership were missing. Thus, this dataset was manually completed with the missing information and the filter was applied using the new manually added information. In Figure 3.7 one can see three performance curves: one for the plain tensor factorization model (PITF-BPR or CD-BPR), one for the factorization model plus the filter version on the original dataset and finally one for the method with filter on the manually enriched version of the dataset.

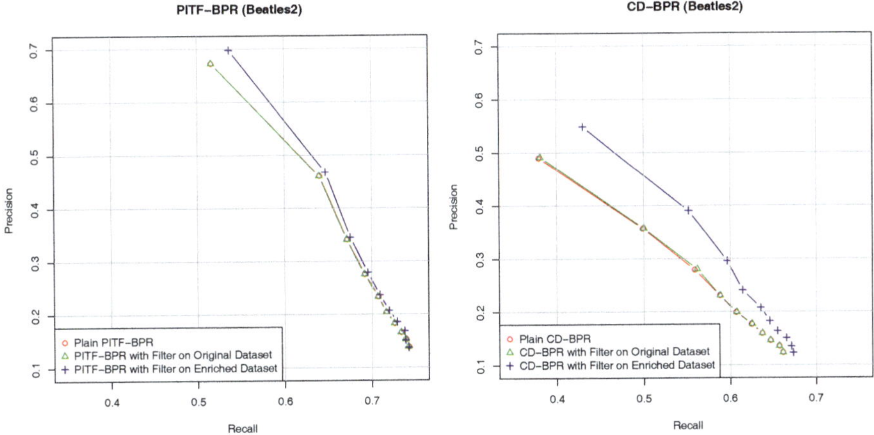

Figure 3.7: Comparison of the filters with and without annotations against the plain tensor factorization through PITF-BPR and CD-BPR. Note that plain PITF-BPR performs better than the filtered CD-BPR.

In Figure 3.7 one can see that, without the annotations, the filter does not lead to a significant performance improvement, which can be seen on the filter on the annotated dataset. From this results it is possible to see that PITF-BPR performs much closer to its filtered version than the CD-BPR method. By modeling explicitly the pairwise relationships between subjects and objects and between predicates and objects, PITF alone is able to capture most of the information used by the filter, and that is why the improvements are not as big as in CD-BPR. It is also important to stress that the performance improvement obtained with the filter came after a considerable amount of tedious and error prone work on manually annotating the dataset. The closeness of the performance of the unfiltered PITF-BPR and the filtered ones suggests that this model is capable of capturing most of the information necessary to provide reasonable answers to the queries.

3.5 Conclusions

In this chapter we have provided empirical evidence that (i) other aspects of the model kept constant, modeling pairwise interactions can lead to better predictive performance and (ii) optimizing the models for a loss function that considers the open world semantics of RDF (where nothing can be said about the truth value of triples not in the dataset) is a more appropriate approach for this task than considering that triples not in the dataset are false. We have shown that the PITF and CD models, when optimized for BPR, are able to provide reasonable predictions of triples that are true in the real world. It can be seen from the experiments that the quality of the results of those models can be improved by completing the datasets with some additional information with which some RDF reasoning can be made. However, the improvement (especially for the PITF model) was not significant compared to the cost of manually completing the datasets. This suggests that the pairwise interactions explicitly modeled by PITF do play an important role on RDF triple truth value prediction.

Chapter 4

Target-Specific Parametrization of Multi-Relational Models

Contents

One of the open problems identified in Chapter 2 is how to properly optimize a factorization model for a number of different target relations. State-of-the-art models discussed in Chapter 2 either (i) are optimized for one single target relation and use the information about the other relations for regularizing the parameters or (ii) learn one set of parameters that represent the optimal compromise on the performance on all target relations. Ideally, however, one is interested in finding optimal models for each target relation individually. This chapter proposes a first step in this direction.

4.1 Learning with multiple target relations

A number of factorization models (Krohn-Grimberghe *et al.*, 2012; Ma *et al.*, 2008; Singh & Gordon, 2008b; Zhang *et al.*, 2010) define one single relation for which predictions should be made, called the **target** relation, while the other relations are used as side information (**auxiliary** relations). Consider for instance the scenario of online social networks, such as Facebook, YouTube, or Flickr, which encourage users to create connections between themselves or to interesting items (e.g., songs, videos, or pictures). The social information (connection between users) can be exploited by recommender systems to provide better recommendations of items of interest (Krohn-Grimberghe *et al.*, 2012) (connections between users and items).

However, in scenarios with many potential target relations, a more interesting model class is required in order to make predictions for all targets, e.g., in the context of recommender systems, a single model that is capable not only of making predictions for the user-item relation based on the user-user one, but also vice versa. Another example of a task where this is important is the mining of Linked Open Data (LOD) bases like DBPedia, for instance supporting probabilistic queries on such databases and providing estimates of facts that are neither explicitly stated in the knowledge base nor can be inferred from logical entailment (Drumond *et al.*, 2012; Nickel *et al.*, 2012). Optimizing the predictions for a number of relations can be seen as a prediction task with multiple target variables. State-of-the-art factorization models approach the problem by sharing the parameters used for predicting all target relations. Instances of such approaches are discussed in Chapter 2 and include RESCAL (Nickel *et al.*, 2011, 2012), MOF-SRP (Jenatton *et al.*, 2012) and SME (Glorot *et al.*, 2013), which share entity specific parameters among all relations in the data. This way, the best solution for the optimization problem is a compromise of the performance on all relations. Although most of these models have been evaluated on multi-target settings, none of them have explicitly investigated the problem of how to optimize each target relation individually, instead of learning the optimal performance compromise on all relations.

To this end, the *Coupled Auxiliary and Target Specific features Multi-target Factorization* (CATSMF) is introduced. CATSMF is a framework for learning multi-relational models which takes into account the possibility that any relation in the data can be a target relation. It defines predictive and auxiliary roles to the parameters and uses a different parametrization of the prediction function for each target relation which are coupled with each other by sharing auxiliary parameters during learning. Having target specific parameters allows CATSMF optimize the parameters for each target relation individually, whereas the shared auxiliary parameters helps to regularize the target specific ones using the information about the other relations. Experiments on real world datasets show that CATSMF improves the predictive performance over the state-of-the-art by modeling such target-specific parameters per relation. This is the first work to introduce a multi-relational factorization approach that fully exploits specific parametrization for different target relations.

In summary, the main contributions of this chapter are:

1. Propose a new factorization approach that optimizes directly for a number of target relations. The novelty of this approach lies in the fact that, for the same entities, we use different parameters when making predictions for different target relations;

2. Show that coupling the models for different target relations, by introducing shared parameters for reconstructing relations when they play an auxiliary role, leads to a more memory efficient method and even to better predictive accuracy;

3. Empirically show the advantage of having specific predictive parameters on different relations to the overall loss. Our experiments on real world datasets demonstrate that CATSMF outperforms state-of-the-art factorization models and has lower runtime.

4.2 Multi-Target Factorization

A number of variants of factorization models for SRL have been proposed in the literature (see Chapter 2 and Table 2.4). CMF (Singh & Gordon, 2008b) assumes that there is one target relation for which predictions should be made while the others comprise side information, and is optimized for the target relation by downweighting the contribution of the others to the overall loss. It is reasonable however to expect that predictions should be made for a different number of relations, i.e., a number of relations in the data can be regarded as target relations, as in the case of the LOD scenario.

Other approaches have been evaluated on multi-target scenarios. For instance, RESCAL (Nickel *et al.*, 2011, 2012), considers the data as a three way tensor, in which the first two modes represent the entities, and the third one, the relations. By factorizing the tensor RESCAL is able to make predictions to all relations. Jenatton *et al.* (2012) go into the same direction. Unlike RESCAL, their model considers both pairwise and three-wise interactions between entities and relations when reconstructing the tensor. This idea is a further development of the Semantic Matching Energy (SME) model introduced by Glorot *et al.* (2013). However all of these models are concerned with a general parametrization for multi-relational factorization. By optimizing a loss in the form of Equation 2.9, a single set of parameters with the overall best average performance over the target relations is learned. However, the problem addressed in this chapter is how to learn such models such that they are optimized for each target relation individually.

Broadly related to our prediction task of target relations is the work on co-ranking for entities and relations in multi-relational data. For instance, Ng *et al.* (2011) propose a framework to determine the importance of both entities and relations simultaneously based on a stationary probability distribution computed from multi-relational data.

4.2.1 Optimizing models for Multiple Target Relations

In state-of-the-art methods, the parameters are learned in such a way that they are optimized for the best performance compromise over all relations and not for the best performance on each relation individually. To see how this is suboptimal for a general model class, let φ be the set of model parameters and $y_r(\cdot; \varphi)$ a prediction model for relation r parametrized with φ. Also, let the set of parameters with the best prediction performance on relation r be denoted by φ_r^*. Such parameters are defined as:

$$\varphi_r^* := \arg\min_{\varphi} L_r(D_r, \hat{y}_r(\cdot; \varphi)).$$

Now, suppose the data comprise two distinct relations, namely r and s, both of them being target ones. State-of-the-art models discussed in Chapter 2 solve a problem like

$$\varphi^* := \arg\min_{\varphi} \left(L_r(D_r, \hat{y}_r(\cdot; \varphi)) + L_s(D_s, \hat{y}_s(\cdot; \varphi)) \right).$$

Now one would expect that $\varphi_r^* \neq \varphi_s^*$. However, by optimizing an objective function like in Equation 2.9 one is constrained to solutions of the form $\varphi_r = \varphi_s = \varphi^*$.

By definition,

$$L_r(D_r, \hat{y}_r(\cdot; \varphi_r^*)) \leq L_r(D_r, \hat{y}_r(\cdot; \varphi^*)) \text{ and } L_s(D_s, \hat{y}_s(\cdot; \varphi_s^*)) \leq L_s(D_s, \hat{y}_s(\cdot; \varphi^*))$$

from which it follows that

$$L_r(D_r, \hat{y}_r(\cdot; \varphi_r^*)) + L_s(D_s, \hat{y}_s(\cdot; \varphi_s^*)) \leq L_r(D_r, \hat{y}_r(\cdot; \varphi^*)) + L_s(D_s, \hat{y}_s(\cdot; \varphi^*)).$$

This means that using parameters optimized specifically for each target relation is, in the *worst* case, at least as good as having one common set of parameters optimized for all relations. Thus a more appropriate solution is to learn one model for each target relation, an approach that we call *Decoupled Target Specific Features Multi-Target Factorization* or *DMF*:

$$\varphi_r^* := \arg\min_{\varphi_r} L_r(D_r, \hat{y}_{r,r}(\cdot; \varphi_r)) + \alpha_{r,s} L_s(D_s, \hat{y}_{r,s}(\cdot; \varphi_r))$$

$$\varphi_s^* := \arg\min_{\varphi_s} L_s(D_s, \hat{y}_{s,s}(\cdot; \varphi_s)) + \alpha_{s,r} L_r(D_r, \hat{y}_{s,r}(\cdot; \varphi_s))$$

with $0 \leq \alpha_{r,s} \leq 1$ and $0 \leq \alpha_{s,r} \leq 1$ and predict using $\hat{y}_{r,r}(\cdot; \varphi_r^*)$ for relation r and $\hat{y}_{s,s}(\cdot; \varphi_s^*)$ for relation s.

More generally, let $\hat{y}_{t,r}$ denote the prediction function for a given relation r when another relation t is the target. The loss function of multi-target factorization models can be written as follows:

$$J(\{\varphi_t\}_{t \in 1,\dots,R}) := \sum_{t=1}^{R} \left(\sum_{r=1}^{R} \alpha_{t,r} L_r(D_r, \hat{y}_{t,r}(D_r; \varphi_t)) + \lambda_t ||\varphi_t||^2 \right) \tag{4.1}$$

Predictions for unseen data points are done using $\hat{y}_t := \hat{y}_{t,t}$. The functions $\hat{y}_{t,r}$ for $r \neq t$ are called auxiliary reconstructions of relation r for the target relation t. L_r is the loss on relation r, as defined in Section 2.1 and $\alpha_{t,r}$ is the importance of relation r when relation t is the target, such that $\alpha_{t,t} = 1$ and $0 \leq \alpha_{t,r} \leq 1$.

Depending on the underlying model, the prediction function $\hat{y}_{t,r}$ can be parametrized in a number of ways. For the purposes of this work, DMF associates one latent feature vector $\varphi_r(x)$ with each instance x for each relation $r = 1, \dots, R$. Accordingly, different feature matrices $\Phi_{t,r}$ are associated with each relation $r = 1, \dots, R$, one per target $t = 1, \dots, R$. The prediction function for DMF is given by Equation 4.2.

$$\hat{y}_{t,r}(x_1, x_2) := \varphi_t(x_1)^\top \Phi_{t,r} \varphi_t(x_2) \tag{4.2}$$

The DMF loss decomposes over t and each component can be optimized independently of each other; this is equivalent to R independent models, one for each target relation. Another point worth noting is that the $\alpha_{t,r}$ relation weights are crucial for this model, e.g., setting all of them to 1 is the same as learning the same model R times (up to a random initialization).

To make this argument more clear, let us revisit the social media example from Chapter 2. In that example there are two entity types, namely users U and news items N and three relations: follows $F := U \times U$, the social relationship $S := U \times U$ and the product consumption (reading of news items) $C := U \times N$. A state-of-the-art multi-factorization model like, for instance RESCAL, would define latent features for users $\varphi(U)$, news items $\varphi(N)$ as well as for the relations Φ_F, Φ_S and Φ_C and learn them as in Equation 4.3 (regularization terms are omitted here to avoid clutter).

$$
\begin{aligned}
(\varphi^*(U), \varphi^*(N), \Phi_F^*, \Phi_S^*, \Phi_C^*) := \underset{\varphi(U),\varphi(N),\Phi_F,\Phi_S,\Phi_C}{\arg\min} \; & L_F(D_F, \hat{y}_F(\cdot; \varphi(U), \Phi_F)) \\
& + L_S(D_S, \hat{y}_S(\cdot; \varphi(U), \Phi_S)) \\
& + L_C(D_C, \hat{y}_C(\cdot; \varphi(U), \varphi(N), \Phi_C))
\end{aligned}
\tag{4.3}
$$

This way, the same user features $\varphi^*(U)$ are used for making predictions for all relations and thus we will refer to this strategy as **complete sharing**. Now, suppose one uses different latent features for different target relations and $\varphi_F(U)$, $\varphi_S(U)$, $\varphi_C(U)$ denote the user features used for making predictions for relations F, S and C respectively. This way it would be possible to learn features such that

$$
\begin{aligned}
\varphi_F^*(U) &:= \underset{\varphi(U)}{\arg\min} \, L_F(D_F, \hat{y}_F(\cdot; \varphi(U), \Phi_F)) \\
\varphi_S^*(U) &:= \underset{\varphi(U)}{\arg\min} \, L_S(D_S, \hat{y}_S(\cdot; \varphi(U), \Phi_S)) \\
\varphi_C^*(U) &:= \underset{\varphi(U)}{\arg\min} \, L_C(D_C, \hat{y}_C(\cdot; \varphi(U), \varphi(N), \Phi_C))
\end{aligned}
$$

while models that follow the *complete sharing* strategy and learn parameters like in Equation 4.3 are constrained to solutions of the form

$$
\varphi_F(U) = \varphi_S(U) = \varphi_C(U) = \varphi^*(U).
$$

However, when learning the parameters for a given relation, it is important to exploit the information about the other relations. Thus, we can reformulate the multi-target factorization problem as a set of single target problems, one for each target relation. This way, the parameters for relation F acting as a target relation are learned as:

$$
\begin{aligned}
(\varphi_F^*(U), \Phi_F^*) := \arg\min_{\varphi_F(U), \Phi_F} & L_F(D_F, \hat{y}_{F,F}(\cdot; \varphi_F(U), \Phi_{F,F})) \\
&+ \alpha_{F,S} L_S(D_S, \hat{y}_{F,S}(\cdot; \varphi_F(U), \Phi_{F,S})) \\
&+ \alpha_{F,C} L_C(D_C, \hat{y}_{F,C}(\cdot; \varphi_F(U), \varphi_F(N), \Phi_{F,C})) \,.
\end{aligned}
$$

The same way, when relation S is the target, the model looks like

$$
\begin{aligned}
(\varphi_S^*(U), \Phi_S^*) := \arg\min_{\varphi_S(U), \Phi_S} & L_S(D_S, \hat{y}_{S,S}(\cdot; \varphi_S(U), \Phi_{S,S})) \\
&+ \alpha_{S,F} L_F(D_F, \hat{y}_{S,F}(\cdot; \varphi_S(U), \Phi_{S,F})) \\
&+ \alpha_{S,C} L_C(D_C, \hat{y}_{S,C}(\cdot; \varphi_S(U), \varphi_S(N), \Phi_{F,C}))
\end{aligned}
$$

Analogously, the same is done for relation C. Since there are three relations, each user $u \in U$ and product $p \in P$ is associated with three latent feature vectors, each corresponding to the case where each relation acts as target. This can be seen in Figure 4.1. There one can see that when one relation acts as a target the other ones are useful for regularizing the parameters for predicting it. Since the *follows* (F) relation is a relation between users and users, one does not need the feature vectors of products $\varphi_F(p)$ for *predicting* it. However, these parameters are useful when *learning* user features $\varphi_F(u)$ since product features are needed to regularize user features using the *consumes* (C) relation. Hence we dub such parameters *auxiliary parameters*. In Figure 4.1, predictive parameters are depicted in a darker blue color and the auxiliary ones in a lighter gray.

4.2.2 Coupled Auxiliary and Target Specific Factorization

One issue with DMF is that the number of parameters to be learned grows by a factor R of the number of relations in the dataset. When relation feature vectors are used, DMF has in total $R^2 k + R|\mathcal{E}|k$ many parameters. This is of course undesirable from the scalability point of view. Furthermore, the fact that individual models are completely decoupled from each other prevents that one benefits from the learning process of the other. To tackle both issues, we propose to couple the models by sharing the parameters used for auxiliary relations. We call

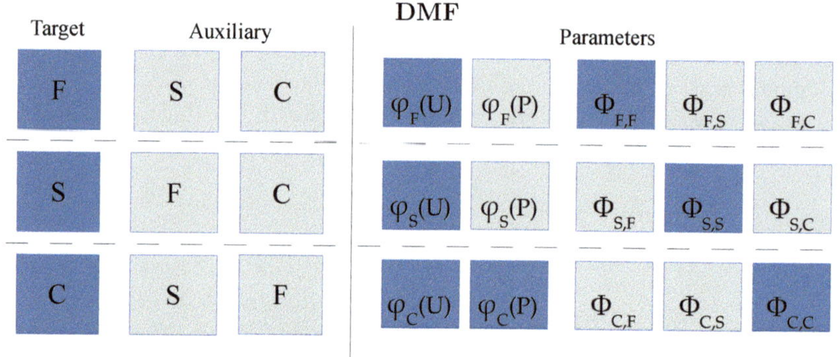

Figure 4.1: DMF parameters for the social media example. In this example there are three relations: *follows* F, *social* S and *consumes* C between two entities *users* U and *products* P. On the left side you see the data in the three cases for which relation acting as a target. On the right side the respective parameters are depicted.

this approach the **Coupled Auxiliary and Target Specific features Multi-target Factorization (CATSMF)** and it represents our core contribution in this chapter. The prediction function for CATSMF is as follows:

$$\hat{y}_{t,r}(x_1, x_2) := \varphi_{t \cdot \delta(x_1 \in \mathcal{E}_t^{(1)})}(x_1)^\top \Phi_{r, \delta(t=r)} \varphi_{t \cdot \delta(x_2 \in \mathcal{E}_t^{(2)})}(x_2) \tag{4.4}$$

where $\mathcal{E}_r^{(1)} \subseteq \mathcal{E}$ and $\mathcal{E}_r^{(2)} \subseteq \mathcal{E}$ are the sets of entities that possibly could occur as the subjects and the objects, respectively, of relation r, as defined in Section 2.1. This means that entities possibly occurring within the target relation t are associated with target specific features φ_t, while entities that do not occur within the target relation t are associated with auxiliary features φ_0 (pooled over all target relations). Every relation r has two feature matrices: one when used as target $\Phi_{r,1}$ and another one when used as auxiliary relation $\Phi_{r,0}$.

CATSMF has two main advantages over DMF: (i) since the auxiliary parameters are shared across the models for different target relations, such models are coupled and can profit from each other. (ii) CATSMF allows for a lower number of parameters. While DMF defines a full set of parameters for each relation, CATSMF defines parameters needed to make the predictions for each target relation, plus one full set of auxiliary ones. For example, if a given entity x does not occur in a relation t, i.e., $x \notin \mathcal{E}_t^{(1)} \cup \mathcal{E}_t^{(2)}$, then $\hat{y}_{t,t}$ is never computed for x and thus $\varphi_t(x)$ is never used and can be dropped. For instance, if r is the relation *father-of*, $\mathcal{E}_r^{(1)}$ and $\mathcal{E}_r^{(2)}$ both correspond to the subset of persons, but not, say, locations, and if r' is the relation *capital-of*, $\mathcal{E}_{r'}^{(1)}$ corresponds to the subset of cities while $\mathcal{E}_{r'}^{(2)}$ corresponds to the subset of countries, but not persons. This means, that for two given entities, a person *John* and location *Berlin*, $\varphi_{\text{capital-of}}(\text{John})$ and $\varphi_{\text{father-of}}(\text{Berlin})$ never have to be computed. Besides leading to a lower number of parameters, taking into consideration entity types can sometimes lead to better predictive performance as observed in Section 4.3.4 among the results of the *Experiment II*.

The number of latent features needed by CATSMF is $2Rk + \sum_{r=1}^{R} |\mathcal{E}_r|k$, where we define $\mathcal{E}_r := \mathcal{E}_r^{(1)} \cup \mathcal{E}_r^{(2)}$ to simplify the notation. The lower $\sum_{r=1}^{R} |\mathcal{E}_r|$, the bigger the savings in the number of parameters. Even in the *worst case scenario*, where there is no entity type information, i.e., if $\mathcal{E}_r = \mathcal{E}$ for all $r = 1, \ldots, R$, the number of parameters required by CATSMF is $2Rk + R|\mathcal{E}|k$. This means that, while the relationship between the number of parameters and the amount of relations is quadratic for DMF, for CATSMF it is linear.

Figure 4.2 shows the CATSMF setup for the social media example. Note how the number of parameters is reduced in comparison to DMF by sharing auxiliary parameters. In Figure 4.1 one can see that there is a lot of redundancy in DMF regarding auxiliary parameters . There are two copies of auxiliary parameters for product features and two copies of each relation auxiliary features. What CATSMF does is essentially to define one set of auxiliary parameters and share them through the cases of different target relations.

CATSMF is learned through a stochastic gradient descent as shown in Algorithm 3. The algorithm starts by initializing the parameters, drawing them from a 0-mean normal distribution (lines 2–7). Then a target relation t is uniformly sampled and a stochastic gradient descent update is made in one observation of t (lines 9–10) according to Algorithm 4. Finally, another relation r is uniformly sampled and an update on this relation, acting as an auxiliary relation for t, is performed (lines 11–12). We do this oversampling of target specific parameters to guarantee that they are more often updated than auxiliary ones, which leads to faster empirical convergence. This process is repeated until convergence.

The parameter update is described in Algorithm 4. First an observation $(x_1, x_2, y) \in D_r$ is uniformly sampled (line 2). The next step is to determine the parameters to estimate $\hat{y}_{t,r}(x_1, x_2)$ that will be updated (lines 3, 5 and 7). If $r = t$, then it plays a target relation role and only the target specific parameters regarding t, namely $\Phi_{t,1}$, $\varphi_t(x_1)$ and $\varphi_t(x_2)$ are updated. In case $r \neq t$, then r plays the role of an auxiliary relation. In this case the auxiliary features $\Phi_{r,0}$ are

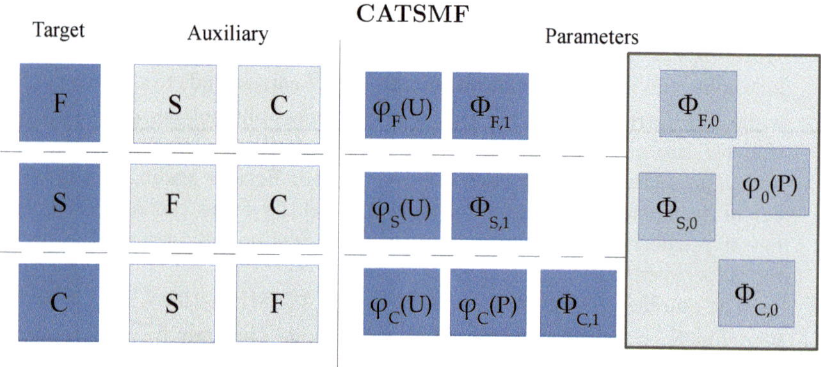

Figure 4.2: CATSMF parameters for the social media example. In this example there are three relations: *follows* F, *social* S and *consumes* C between two entities *users* U and *products* P. On the left side you see the data in the three cases for which relation acting as a target. On the right side the respective parameters are depicted. Please note that the auxiliary parameters are shared across the target relations.

used. If x_1 is among the entities related by t, i.e., $x_1 \in \mathcal{E}_t$, then $\varphi_t(x_1)$ is used, otherwise the auxiliary features $\varphi_0(x_1)$ are in place. We proceed analogously for x_2. Finally, the chosen parameters are updated with a stochastic gradient descent step (lines 4, 6 and 8).

4.2.3 Setting up CATSMF

Often overlooked in the multi-relational factorization literature are bias terms. We use target-specific and auxiliary bias terms. The prediction function is the following:

$$\hat{y}_{t,r}(x_1, x_2) := b_{r,\delta(t=r)} + b_{t\cdot\delta(x_1 \in \mathcal{E}_t)}(x_1) + b_{t\cdot\delta(x_2 \in \mathcal{E}_t)}(x_2) \qquad (4.5)$$
$$+ \varphi_{t\cdot\delta(x_1 \in \mathcal{E}_t)}(x_1)\Phi_{r,\delta(t=r)}\varphi_{t\cdot\delta(x_1 \in \mathcal{E}_t)}(x_2)$$

where $b_{r,\delta(t=r)}, b_{t\delta(x_1 \in \mathcal{E}_t)}(x_1), b_{t\delta(x_2 \in \mathcal{E}_t)}(x_2)$ are bias terms. The parameters in this prediction function should be optimized for the task at hand, which is to make predictions based on positive only observations.

In Chapter 3 we argue and provide empirical evidence that the BPR optimization criterion (BPR-Opt), proposed by Rendle *et al.* (2009a), is suitable for this

---

Algorithm 3 CATSMF

1: **procedure** LEARNMULTITARGET
    input: number of relations R, training data $\{D_r\}_{r=1,\ldots,R}$, set of entities $\mathcal{E}$, set of entities that possibly could occur in relation r: $\{\mathcal{E}_r\}_{r=1,\ldots,R}$, learning rate η, and regularization constants λ

2:      $\forall_{x\in\mathcal{E}}\ \varphi_0(x) \sim \mathcal{N}(0,\sigma^2)$
3:      **for** $r = 1,\ldots,R$ **do**
4:        $\forall_{x\in\mathcal{E}_r}\ \varphi_r(x) \sim \mathcal{N}(0,\sigma^2)$
5:        $\Phi_{r,0}(x) \sim \mathcal{N}(0,\sigma^2\mathbf{I})$
6:        $\Phi_{r,1}(x) \sim \mathcal{N}(0,\sigma^2\mathbf{I})$
7:      **end for**
8:      **repeat**
9:        $t \sim \mathrm{Uniform}(1,R)$
10:       $(\varphi,\Phi) = \mathrm{UpdateModel}(t,t,D_t,\varphi,\Phi,\eta,\lambda_t)$
11:       $r \sim \mathrm{Uniform}(1,R)$
12:       $(\varphi,\Phi) = \mathrm{UpdateModel}(t,r,D_r,\varphi,\Phi,\eta,\lambda_t)$
13:      **until** convergence
14: **end procedure**

Algorithm 4 CATSMF Stochastic Gradient Descent Update

1: **procedure** UPDATEMODEL
    input: target relation t, auxiliary relation r, observations about relation r: D_r, set of entity features φ, set of relation features Φ, learning rate η, and regularization constant λ_t
    output: updated entity features φ and updated relation features Φ

2:      $(x_1,x_2,y) \sim \mathrm{Uniform}(D_r)$
3:      $r' \leftarrow t\delta(x_1 \in \mathcal{E}_t)$
4:      $\varphi_{r'}(x_1) \leftarrow \varphi_{r'}(x_1) - \eta\left(\frac{\partial \ell_r(y,\hat{y}_{t,r}(x_1,x_2))}{\partial \varphi_{r'}(x_1)} + \lambda_t\varphi_{r'}(x_1)\right)$
5:      $r' \leftarrow t\delta(x_2 \in \mathcal{E}_t)$
6:      $\varphi_{r'}(x_2) \leftarrow \varphi_{r'}(x_2) - \eta\left(\frac{\partial \ell_r(y,\hat{y}_{t,r}(x_1,x_2))}{\partial \varphi_{r'}(x_2)} + \lambda_t\varphi_{r'}(x_2)\right)$
7:      $r' \leftarrow r\delta(t = r)$
8:      $\Phi_{r'} \leftarrow \Phi_{r'} - \eta\left(\frac{\partial \ell_r(y,\hat{y}_{t,r}(x_1,x_2))}{\partial \Phi_{r'}} + \lambda_t\Phi_{r'}\right)$
9:      **return** (φ,Φ)
10: **end procedure**

---

task. Equation 3.4 in Chapter 3 formalizes BPR-Opt for the problem of RDF triple prediction. Be $\sigma(x) = \frac{1}{1+e^{-x}}$ the sigmoid function, BPR-Opt is an instance of a pairwise loss and can be defined for a general multi-relational learning task as follows:

$$\text{BPR-Opt}_r(D_r, \hat{y}_{t,r}) := \sum_{(x_1, x_2, 1) \in D_r^{\text{train}}}$$

$$\sum_{(x_1, x_2', 1) \in \mathcal{X}_r \times \{1\} \setminus D_r^{\text{train}}} \ln \sigma(\hat{y}_{t,r}(x_1, x_2) - \hat{y}_{t,r}(x_1, x_2')).$$

4.3 Evaluation

In this section, CATSMF and DMF are compared against each other and against state-of-the-art baselines. More specifically, we examine the impact of using target specific parameters as well as of considering target and auxiliary roles for relations.

The evaluation is divided into two experiments. The first one, *Experiment I*, assesses the performance of the approach proposed here on three benchmark datasets for multi-relational learning tasks. The datasets used in this experiment are well studied and widely used for evaluation of relational learning approaches. The goal of this experiment is to determine whether CATSMF is able to achieve state-of-the-art performance on those standard and relatively well solved problems. The second experiment, *Experiment II*, analyzes the behavior of CATSMF on practical Web applications using three larger Web datasets. The datasets used for both experiments are summarized in Table 4.1.

In the following, the the state-of-the-art baselines used in the experiments are presented as well as the evaluation protocol and then the results of the empirical study are shown in detail.

4.3.1 Comparison against the state-of-the-art

As far as the approach proposed here is concerned we want to make sure that any effects observed come from the usage of predictive and auxiliary features and not from a specific loss or how relation feature matrices look like. Thus three variants of the same prediction model are evaluated. They are detailed as follows:

- **Shared-Diag-BPR** uses the *complete sharing* strategy. This is how state-of-the-art methods approach model parametrization. **Shared-Diag-BPR**

Table 4.1: **Dataset Statistics**

Dataset	$|\mathcal{E}|$	R	$\sum_r^R |D_r|$
Benchmarks			
Kinships	104	26	10,790
UMLS	135	49	6,752
Nations	125	57	3,106
Web			
DBpedia	269,862	5	625,680
Wikipedia-SVO	30,605	4,547	1,300,000
BlogCatalog	10,351	2	682,442

can be seen as **RESCAL** with a diagonal matrix for relation features and optimized for BPR-Opt instead of the L2 loss.

- **DMF-Diag-BPR** comprises a set of decoupled models (i.e., no parameter sharing between them), one for each target relation as in Equation 4.2.

- **CATSMF-Diag-BPR** is the core contribution of this chapter, that uses the parametrization from Equation 4.5, with target-specific parameters and shared ones for auxiliary relations.

In the experiments here, the proposed approach is compared against the state-of-the-art models **RESCAL** and **MOF-SRP** (see Chapter 2 and Table 2.4 for more details on the models):

- **RESCAL** (Nickel *et al.*, 2011) uses the *complete sharing* strategy and can be described as *Shared-Full-L2*. Makes no use of specific target features and use full matrices for relation features. Specific relations are optimized for the L2 loss;

- **MOF-SRP** (Jenatton *et al.*, 2012) also follows the *complete sharing* strategy and uses full matrices for relation features but represents them by outer products of one dimensional arrays, in order to require less parameters. The model is optimized for the logistic loss. It is important to point out that here the models are evaluated using the *Split and Sample* strategy. This means that the negative examples seen by MOF-SRP (denoted by Jenatton *et al.* (2012) as $\mathcal{N}$) are sampled following the *Split and Sample* strategy as described in Table 2.3, instead of the sampling of negative items used in the original paper. The rationale for this is given in Section 2.3.

Note that both of them use full matrices for relation features and make no use of specific target features. Table 4.2 presents a summary of the approaches evaluated here.

4.3.2 Evaluation Protocol and Metrics

For all experiments presented in this section, the same evaluation protocol was used. The dataset is spit into training, validation, and test set. First, 10% of the positive tuples are randomly selected and assigned to the test set. Then, we randomly sample 10% of the remaining ones to form the validation set. The remaining triples are used for training. To reduce variability, 10-fold cross-validation was performed. The results reported are the average over the rounds considering 99% confidence intervals. For this evaluation, we follow a protocol based on Cremonesi *et al.* (2010) as described next. For each relation r and entity x on the test set:

1. Sample a set $r_x^- \subseteq \{(x, x_2, y) | (x, x_2, y) \notin D_r^{\text{train}} \cup D_r^{\text{test}}\}$, i.e., unobserved triples in the knowledge base.

2. Then, compute the score for the $|r_x^-|$ negative triples and for each of the positive ones $r_x^+ = \{(x, x_2, y) | (x, x_2, y) \in D_r^{\text{test}}\}$ in the test set.

3. Finally, measure the Area under the ROC Curve (AUC) (defined in Equation 4.7), Precision at 5 (as in Equation 3.8) and Recall at 5 (as in Equation 3.9) metrics on this list of triples.

To simplify our notation we define the set of positive observations for a relation r and instance x_1 as

$$x_{1_r}^+ := \{x_2 \mid (x_1, x_2, 1) \in D_r^{\text{test}}\}$$

and the set of negative ones

$$x_{1_r}^- := \{x_2' \mid (x_1, x_2', 0) \in D_r^{\text{test}}\} .$$

For a given relation r, the AUC is defined in Equation 4.6.

$$AUC(r) := \frac{1}{|\mathcal{E}_r|} \sum_{x_1 \in \mathcal{E}_r} \frac{1}{|x_{1_r}^+||x_{1_r}^-|} \sum_{x_2 \in x_{1_r}^+} \sum_{x_2' \in x_{1_r}^-} \delta(\hat{y}(x_1, x_2) > \hat{y}(x_1, x_2')) \qquad (4.6)$$

Table 4.2: **Models used in the CATSMF and DMF evaluation.**

Method	Prediction function $\hat{y}_r(x_1, x_2)$	Relation loss	Relation Features	Target Parameters
RESCAL	$\varphi(x_1)^\top \Phi_r \varphi(x_2)$	L2	Full Matrix	Complete Sharing
MOF-SRP	$\mathbf{a}\Phi_r\mathbf{a}^\top + \varphi(x_1)\Phi_r\mathbf{b}^\top + \mathbf{b}\Phi_r\varphi(x_2)^\top + \varphi(x_1)^\top \Phi_r\varphi(x_2)$	Logistic	$\displaystyle \Phi_r = \sum_{j=1}^{d} w_j^r \mathbf{u}_j \mathbf{v}_j^\top$	Complete Sharing
Shared-Diag-BPR	$b_r + b(x_1) + b(x_2) + \varphi(x_1)^\top \Phi_r \varphi(x_2)$	BPR-Opt	Diagonal Matrix	Complete Sharing
DMF-Diag-BPR	$b_{r,1} + b_r(x_1) + b_r(x_2) + \varphi_t(x_1)^\top \Phi_r \varphi_t(x_2)$	BPR-Opt	Diagonal Matrix	DMF
CATSMF-Diag-BPR	$b_{r,1} + b_r(x_1) + b_r(x_2) + \varphi_{t\delta(x_1\in\mathcal{E}_t)}(x_1)^\top \Phi_{r,\delta(t=r)} \varphi_{t\delta(x_2\in\mathcal{E}_t)}(x_2)$	BPR-Opt	Diagonal Matrix	CATSMF

The total AUC is the average over all relations.

$$AUC := \frac{\sum_{r=1}^{R} AUC(r)}{R} \tag{4.7}$$

For each dataset, split and model the hyperparameters were tuned using the train and validation set through grid-search. Next, the models were retrained on both train and validation sets and evaluated on test partition. The results reported correspond to the performance of the methods on the test set only. This process was performed for *all* the models in the evaluation, including the baselines. Regarding hyperparameter values, the number of latent features k was searched in the range $\{10, 25, 50\}$ for all baselines and variants of our approach. The values for $\alpha_{t,r}$, λ_r and η were searched in $\{0.25, 0.5, 0.75\}$, $\{0.0001, 0.001, 0.01\}$ and $\{0.0005, 0.005, 0.05\}$ respectively. All the hyperparameters for the baselines were searched in the ranges suggested by their respective authors in their papers.

4.3.3 Experiment I: Benchmark Datasets

In this experiment, we show that CATSMF achieves state-of-the-art performance on benchmark datasets for multi-relational learning tasks. The datasets are described and then the experimental results presented.

Datasets

The three benchmark datasets correspond to **Kinships**, **UMLS**, and **Nations** and they are described as follows.

- **Kinships**: depicts the kinship terms used by the members of the Australian Alyawarra tribe to describe each other (Denham, 1973). The dataset has 10,790 triples about 26 kinship relations and 104 entities.

- **UMLS**: contains terms from the Unified Medical Language System. The relationships are 49 verbs depicting causal influence (McCray, 2003) like `complicates` or `affects` among 135 entities (terms). There are 6,752 observed triples.

- **Nations**: represents interactions between countries like `economic_aid` and `treaties` (Rummel, 1999). The dataset has 3,106 triples about 57 relations and 125 entities.

Results and Discussion

Figure 4.3 summarizes the performance of the proposed approach and the state-of-the-art in terms of AUC, Recall at 5, and Precision at 5. We can observe from the figure that our approaches indeed achieve a comparable performance with existing methods on these three benchmark datasets. Note that for these datasets there is almost no significant difference between the methods, since the datasets are small, well studied and the performance achieved is close to the maximum.

It is important to state that, while we report here in Figure 4.3a the area under the ROC curve, Nickel *et al.* (2011) and Jenatton *et al.* (2012) report the area under the Precision-Recall curve but also refer to it as AUC. This explains the different values between the ones reported on Figure 4.3a and the ones reported by Nickel *et al.* (2011) and Jenatton *et al.* (2012).

Due to the number of relations on these datasets, to estimate all $\alpha_{t,r}$ values through grid-search is infeasible. Because of that, we set them to $\alpha_{t,t} = 1$ and $\alpha_{t,r} = a$, where a is a hyperparameter estimated on validation data using grid search. We did the same to the regularization constants, setting all $\lambda_t = \lambda$.

Figure 4.3a shows the results for AUC where we can observe that, although CATSMF uses less parameters than DMF there is no significant difference on the performance of both methods. The same can be observed in the results for Recall at 5 and Precision at 5 in Figure 4.3b and Figure 4.3c, respectively. A summary of the statistically significant winners can be found on Table 4.3.

4.3.4   Experiment II: Web Datasets

The second experiment analyzes the performance of our approach on three larger Web datasets collected from DBpedia, Wikipedia, and BlogCatalog. Here we want to assert the usefulness of our approach on concrete real world applications. In this experiments we apply the models described here to LOD mining, natural language processing and recommender systems. On top of that, since two of the datasets have a lower number of relations we are able to better investigate the impact of having target-specific parameters.

DBpedia is one of the central interlinking-hubs of the emerging Web of Data[1], which makes it really attractive to evaluate multi-relational learning approaches. The Wikipedia-SVO dataset has the highest number of relations among published multi-relational datasets (Jenatton *et al.*, 2012). The BlogCatalog dataset (Tang

---

[1] `http://lod-cloud.net`

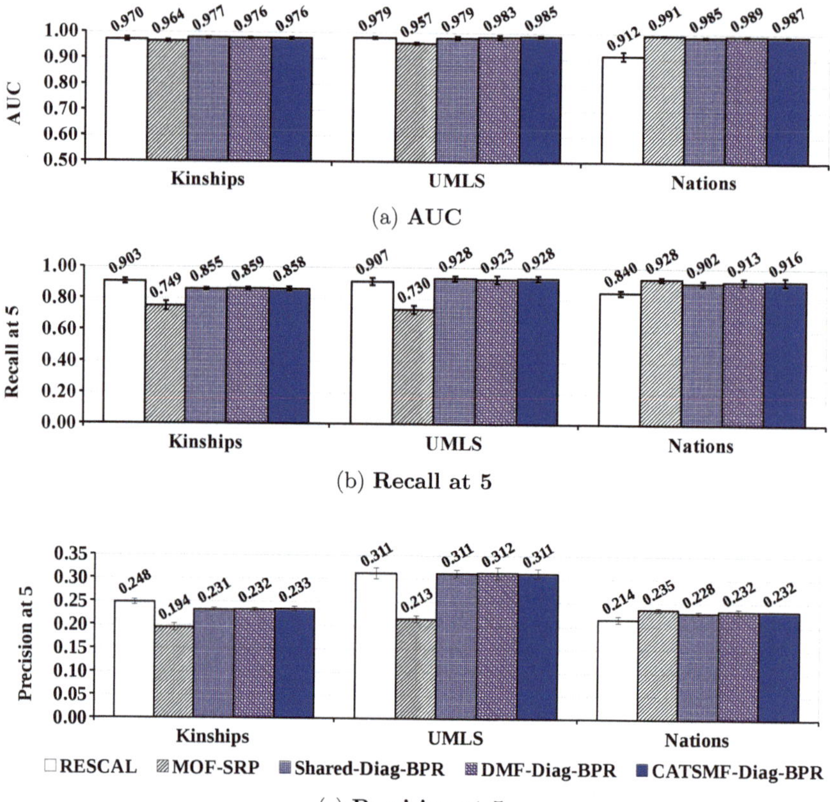

(a) **AUC**

(b) **Recall at 5**

(c) **Precision at 5**

Figure 4.3: Performance on benchmark datasets used in *Experiments I*.

& Liu, 2009a) has been used in the literature to evaluate recommender systems that exploit social network information (Krohn-Grimberghe *et al.*, 2012; Tang & Liu, 2009a,b) as in our running example in Chapter 2.

Datasets

The Web datasets for the evaluation are detailed as follows:

Table 4.3: **Summary of the statistically significant winners for the Benchmark Datasets. Cells in boldface indicate that CATSMF is the winner alone. Italic ones indicate a tie with CATSMF among the winners.**

Dataset	AUC		Recall		Precision	
Kinships	*RESCAL,*	*Shared-DMF,*	RESCAL		RESCAL	
	Diag,					
	CATSMF					
UMLS	*RESCAL,*	*Shared-DMF,*	*RESCAL,*	*Shared-DMF,*	*RESCAL,*	*Shared-DMF,*
	BPR,		*BPR,*		*BPR,*	
	CATSMF		*CATSMF*		*CATSMF*	
Nations	MOF-SRP, DMF		*MOF-SRP,*	*Shared-DMF,*	*MOF-SRP,*	*Shared-DMF,*
			BPR,		*BPR,*	
			CATSMF		*CATSMF*	

- **DBpedia**: sample of 625,680 triples from the *DBpedia Properties* in English[1]. It consists of 269,862 entities and 5 relations regarding the music domain. Such relations are: `associated_band`, `associated_musical_artist`, `composer`, `artist` and `genre`.

- **Wikipedia-SVO** (Jenatton *et al.*, 2012): depicts subject-verb-object triples extracted from over two million Wikipedia articles, where the verbs play the role of the relationship. It consists of 1,300,000 triples about 4,547 relationships and 30,605 entities.

- **BlogCatalog** (Tang & Liu, 2009a): BlogCatalog[2] is a large blogging website with social network features. The dataset consists of two relations, with one relation between users and blogs indicating which blogs the users find interested and the social relation between users and other users. The task at hand is to recommend both interesting blogs and potential new friends to users. Note that previous work on this dataset (Krohn-Grimberghe *et al.*, 2012; Tang & Liu, 2009a,b) focused on the single target task of using the social information to recommend blogs. There is a total of 10,312 users and 39 blogs.

---

[1]`http://downloads.dbpedia.org/3.6/`
[2]`http://www.blogcatalog.com/`

Table 4.4: **Summary of the statistically significant winners for the Web Datasets. Cells in boldface indicate that CATSMF is the winner alone.**

Dataset	AUC	Recall	Precision
DBpedia	**CATSMF**	MOF-SRP	MOF-SRP
Wikipedia-SVO	**CATSMF**	**CATSMF**	**CATSMF**
BlogCatalog	**CATSMF**	**CATSMF**	**CATSMF**

Results and Discussion

In the DBpedia and BlogCatalog datasets we set $\alpha_{t,t} = 1$ and estimated both the other $\alpha_{t,r}$ and the λ_t values through grid search. For Wikipedia-SVO we proceeded as for the benchmark datasets in *Experiment I*. Here the results are shown in two different figures. Figure 4.4 shows how CATSMF performs against the state-of-the-art baselines while Figure 4.5 compares CATSMF-Diag-BPR against its variations Shared-Diag-BPR and DMF-Diag-BPR.

In the larger and more challenging DBpedia dataset, our approach, CATSMF, clearly outperforms RESCAL in all measures and MOF-SRP in AUC. CATSMF has clearly the best performance in the Wikipedia-SVO dataset.[1] Finally, for the BlogCatalog dataset, one can see that our approaches outperform RESCAL and MOF-SRP. The winners on each dataset and measure considering 99% confidence intervals can be seen on Table 4.4. We believe that the poor performance of RESCAL on the BlogCatalog dataset is due to the optimization for the squared error since it has been observed that models optimized for the BPR loss perform much better on this particular dataset (Krohn-Grimberghe *et al.*, 2012). Combining experiments I and II, three performance measures were evaluated on 6 datasets, giving a total of 18 experiments. Out of those 18 tests, CATSMF was the sole winner on 7 of then and among the winners of 6 ties. RESCAL on the other hand was the sole winner on 2 of them as well as MOF-SRP. In experiment II CATSMF was the sole winner on 7 out of 9 trials with the more challenging Web datasets. Furthermore we would like to point out that the improvements of DMF and CATSMF over the Shared-Diag approach observed in Figure 4.5 are statistically significant.

---

[1]In addition to the results reported here, we reproduced the same experiment on the Wikipedia-SVO dataset performed by Jenatton *et al.* (2012), where the hit rate at the top 5% (referred in their paper as p@5) and 20% (referred to in the original paper as p@20) is measured. CATSMF achieves a p@5 of 0.74 and a p@20 of 0.95, while MOF-SRP is reported to achieve 0.75 and 0.95 respectively.

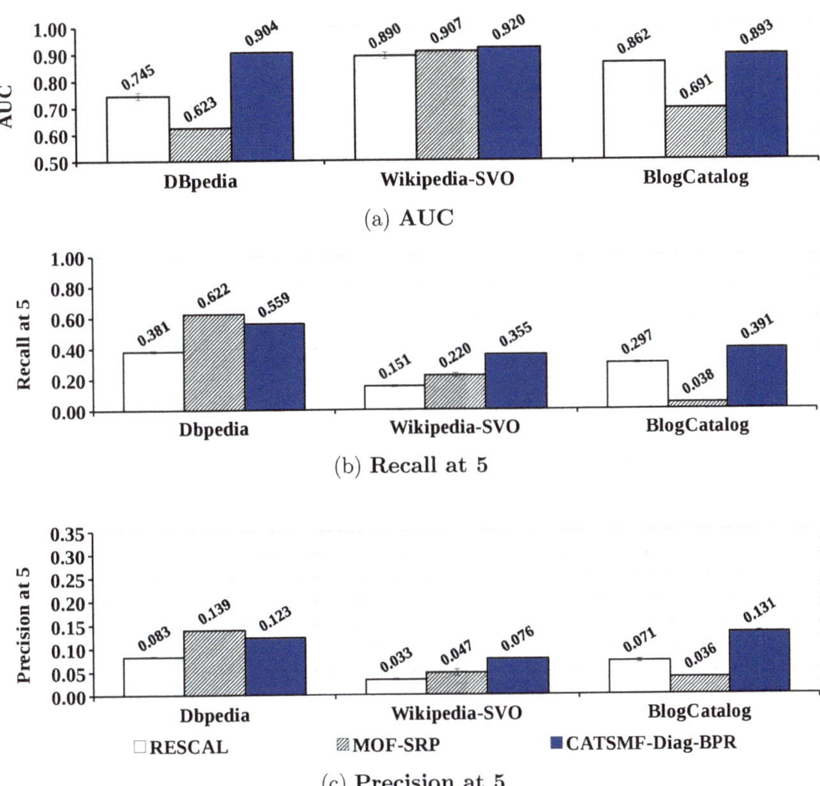

Figure 4.4: Performance of CATSMF against state-of-the-art baselines on the Web datasets used in *Experiments II*.

We observe that MOF-SRP does not exhibit a good performance on the BlogCatalog dataset. One possible explanation is that this model does not take into account entity type information. This means that when learning on the User-Blog relation, the MOF-SRP assumes that users are also potential items to be recommended. As reported by Jenatton *et al.* (2012), negative examples are sampled when learning the model, but since it does not differentiate between *users* and *blogs* and there are 10,312 users and only 39 blogs, one can expect that approximately 99.6% of the sampled negative examples are trivial ones containing recommendations of users. One can see it when looking into the performance

71

on the individual relations. On the social User-User relation, MOF-SRP achieves 0.901 AUC against 0.961 AUC of CATSMF. On the User-Blog relation however the AUC for MOF-SRP is 0.481 against 0.825 of CATSMF. These results suggest MOF-SRP was not able to learn accurately the information abput entity types for this dataset.

Impact of target specific parameters

When analyzing the results from Figure 4.3 we observe that our approach exhibits state-of-the-art performance in the benchmark datasets and excels in the larger ones as seen in Figure 4.4. However, it is hard to reach any conclusions as to which aspects of the models are responsible for the relative differences in performance, since the models evaluated use different parametrization, prediction, and loss functions. Therefore, to answer the question: *what is the impact on prediction performance of using target specific parameters, while using the same prediction function and the same relation specific losses?* we can take a closer look at Shared-Diag-BPR, DMF-Diag-BPR, and CATSMF-Diag-BPR on the DBpedia and BlogCatalog datasets as shown in Figure 4.5.

The results show that using target specific parameters improves over the complete parameter sharing scenario while using both shared and target specific parameters gives an even stronger performance boost. As expected, the differences for Recall@5 and Precision@5 are even greater than the ones for AUC. It is important to note that RESCAL and MOF-SRP also can be used within the target specific parameter framework offered by CATSMF and DMF.

Runtime

Here we report the average runtime over 10 runs on the DBpedia dataset on a Xeon E5620 2.40GHz CPU. As seen in Figure 4.6, the average duration is 754 seconds for CATSMF-Diag-BPR, 7460.3 seconds for RESCAL and 77406.25 secs or, approximately, 21 hours for MOF-SRP on the DBpedia dataset, which shows that CATSMF-Diag-BPR scales much better w.r.t. runtime while providing very competitive prediction performance. There are two main reasons that can explain the better runtime performance of CATSMF-Diag-BPR: (i) the fact that CATSMF-Diag-BPR uses a diagonal matrix for relation features whereas RESCAL uses a full matrix and MOF-SRP a matrix represented as outer products of feature vectors and (ii) we learn CATSMF-Diag-BPR using the scalable stochastic gradient descent learning algorithm.

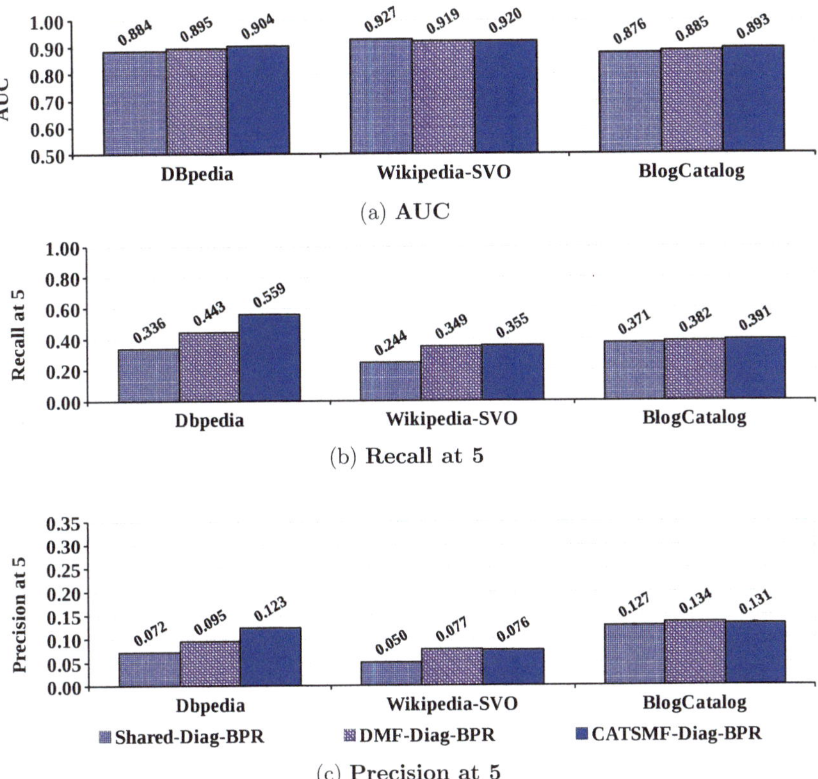

(a) AUC

(b) Recall at 5

(c) Precision at 5

Figure 4.5: Performance on Web datasets used in *Experiments II*.

As discussed in Chapter 2, using a diagonal matrix as relation features may not be the best choice in terms of prediction performance. However, as shown in figures 4.3 and 4.5 the target-specific strategy of CATSMF-Diag-BPR improves the results making it competitive against state-of-the-art models while still having much lower runtime as it can be seen in Figure 4.6. It is important to state that the CATSMF framework can be applied to any model, RESCAL and MOF-SRP included.

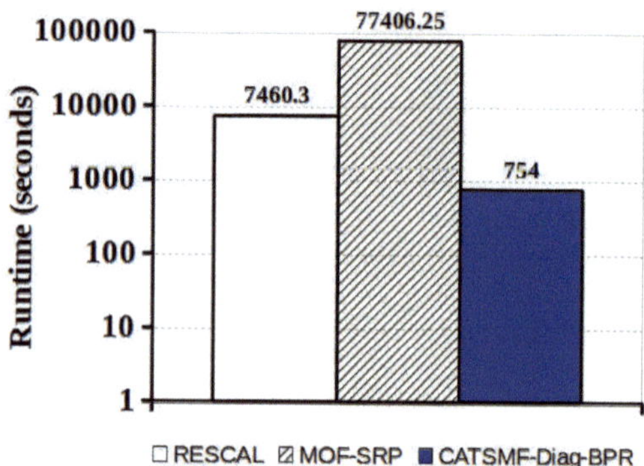

Figure 4.6: Average runtime in seconds on the DBpedia dataset shown in a *logarithmic* scale

Reproducibility of the experiments

DMF and CATSMF were implemented in C++. For RESCAL and MOF-SRP we used implementations provided by the authors. However, to compute RESCAL on the DBPedia dataset we had to use our own implementation of this model since the one provided by the authors did not scale to this dataset. Our implementation was carefully calibrated against the original one on the three benchmark datasets.

4.4   Conclusion

This chapter argued and showed empirically how multi-relational factorization models can benefit from using different parametrizations of prediction functions for different target relations. First a naive set of decoupled models, one for each target relation called DMF, was proposed and then a more memory-efficient variant with shared auxiliary parameters CATSMF, which has less parameters and, thus, scales better. The novelty of DMF and CATSMF lies in the fact that they learn different sets of parameters for reconstructing different target relations. In contrast to the trivial DMF solution of learning one model per target, being all such models completely decoupled from each other, CATSMF defines parameters to be used when a given relation plays an auxiliary role, which are shared among all different models for the various targets.

The experiments have shown that (i) CATSMF is able to scale to large datasets better then state-of-the-art models, while still having competitive predictive performance; (ii) CATSMF and DMF are always at least as good as the standard approach of using the same set of parameters for all target relations, but often outperforming it; (iii) this approach achieves state-of-the-art predictive performance on benchmark relational datasets while outperforming competitor models in tasks like LOD mining, natural language processing and recommender systems.

One interesting direction for future work is to investigate a more memory efficient CATSMF variant, e.g., by reducing the number of parameters to be learned. One possible alternative to this end would be to introduce an ℓ_1 regularizer so as to remove some of the small parameters and trim the model even further.

Chapter 5

Factorization models for Semi-Supervised Classification

Contents

Multi-relational factorization models can be applied to a number of standard machine learning problems. This chapter investigates how to apply them to binary classification, more specifically to semi-supervised classification. When applied to standard classification problems factorization models perform dimensionality reduction in parallel with the learning of the classifier, so that the low-dimensional embeddings exploit the label information. Experiments on real world datasets show that these models are able to outperform state-of-the-art semi-supervised classifiers. The results and findings of this chapter have been published by the author of this thesis in Drumond *et al.* (2014).

5.1 Semi-Supervised Classification

In certain domains, the acquisition of labeled data might be a costly process making it difficult to exploit supervised learning models. In order to surmount this, the field of semi-supervised learning (Chapelle *et al.*, 2006b) studies how to learn from both labeled and unlabeled data. Given the small amount of available labeled data, semi-supervised learning methods need to make strong assumptions about the data distribution. The most prominent assumptions (briefly discussed in Section 2) are the cluster and the manifold assumption.

It is usually the case that, if such assumptions do not hold, unlabeled data may be seriously detrimental to the performance of the algorithm (Cozman *et al.*, 2003). As a consequence, determining in advance good assumptions about the data and developing or choosing models accordingly may be as critical as gathering labeled data. Chapelle *et al.* (2006a) performed an extensive benchmark evaluation of semi-supervised learning approaches on a variety of datasets resulting in no overall winner, i.e. no method is consistently competitive on all datasets, so that one has to rely on background knowledge about the data. General models that can work well on different kinds of data offer a means to circumvent this pitfall. One promising family of models that work in this direction are factorization models (Singh & Gordon, 2008a). Such models are flexible enough to fit different kinds of data without overfitting (given that they are properly regularized). However, there is no systematic evaluation of the capabilities of factorization models as semi-supervised classifiers.

In this chapter, we show how semi-supervised learning can be approached as a multi-relational factorization problem, where both the predictor and the target matrices are collectively decomposed. By factorizing the predictor matrix, one can exploit unlabeled data to learn meaningful latent features together with the decision boundary. This approach however is suboptimal if the data is not linearly separable. Thus, we enforce neighboring points in the original space to still be neighbors in the learned latent space by factorizing also the adjacency matrix of the nearest neighbor graph. We call this model the Predictor/Neighborhood/Target Collective Matrix Factorization (PNT-CMF).

To better illustrate the approach proposed here, we analyze what happens if we apply it to the *Two moons* dataset (Belkin *et al.*, 2006), a toy dataset consisting of 200 instances, each one with 2 predictors. Figure 5.1a depicts the dataset on the original feature space. Figure 5.1b shows the two dimensional latent space and the respective decision boundary learned only on the predictor and target relations, thus completely disregarding the neighborhood relation. The decomposition of the target matrix pushes labeled points from distinct classes away from each other while roughly preserving the same structure as the original space for the unlabeled instances. Thus, it is impossible to find a linear decision boundary that optimally separates the classes. Figure 5.1c shows what happens when we disregard the predictor matrix and rely solely on the neighborhood information. In this case, not only the labeled instances were drawn away from each other, but the neighborhood relationships were preserved. Transitively, the neighborhood of other instances was also preserved. As a consequence, the whole clusters from the two labeled points were pulled away from each other, thus rendering the data linearly separable on the latent space and allowing the model to correctly classify all the instances.

It is important to stress that the *Two Moons* dataset is an extreme case where the neighborhood encodes all information needed to correctly classify the data. For different datasets the neighborhood may encode less useful information and, sometimes, even none. PNT-CMF allows to learn the contribution of the neighborhood and predictors controlled by a hyperparameter. We argue that PNT-CMF is able to perform well on datasets with different underlying structures and distributions and that it is competitive against state-of-the-art supervised and semi-supervised classifiers. While the state-of-the-art approaches may usually be very effective in some datasets, they perform poorly in others; we provide empirical evidence that PNT-CMF can profit from unlabeled data, making them competitive in settings where different model assumptions hold true.

The main contributions of this chapter are:

- The semi-supervised classification problem is formalized as a multi-relational learning problem using the notational framework proposed in Chapter 2;

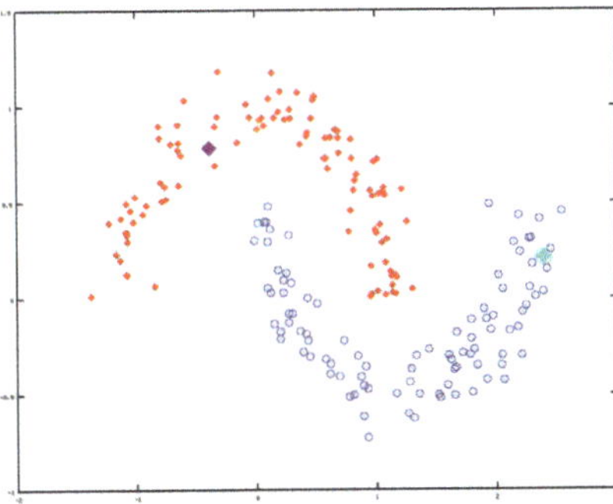

(a) Two Moons data set on the original feature space.

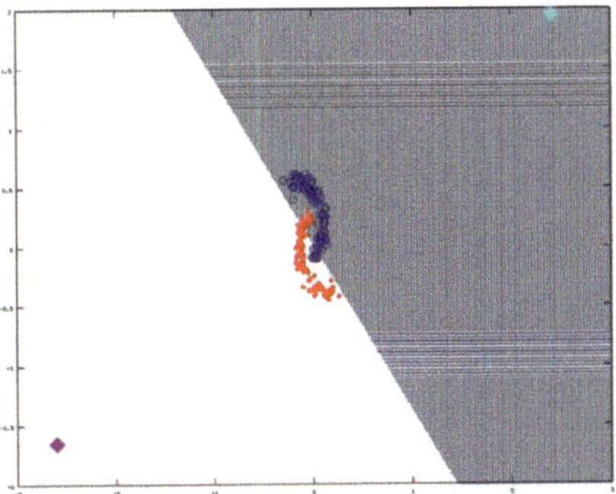

(b) Latent space learned using the *predictors* and *target* matrices.

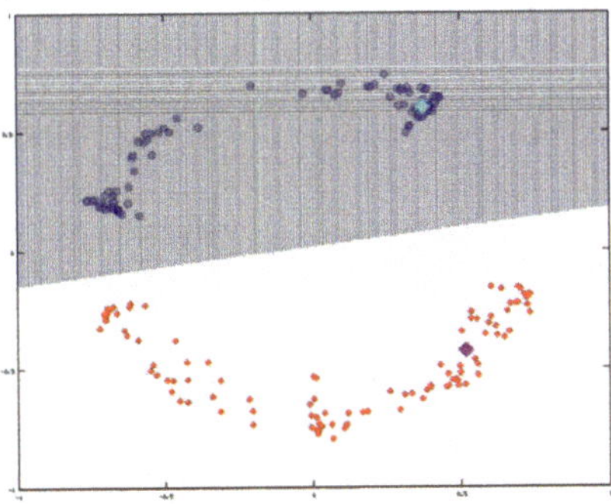

(c) Latent space learned using the *neighborhood* and *target* matrices.

Figure 5.1: Two Moons data set. The points are colored according to their true labels and the labeled training instances are plotted as bigger points in magenta and cyan. The decision function on the latent space figures is the straight line separating the blue and red areas.

- The chapter proposes PNT-CMF, a novel model for semi-supervised learning that collectively factorizes the predictor, neighborhood and target relation.

- A learning algorithm for PNT-CMF is devised. Such algorithm is based on simultaneous stochastic gradient descent over all three relations.

- In experiments on both synthetic and real-world data sets we show that our approach PNT-CMF outperforms existing state-of-the-art methods for semi-supervised learning (TSVM, LapSVM). Especially we show that while existing approaches work well for datasets with matching characteristics (cluster-like datasets for TSVM and manifold-like datasets for LapSVM), our approach PNT-CMF consistently performs competitive under varying characteristics.

5.2 Related Work

5.2.1 Semi-Supervised learning

For a thorough survey of literature on semi-supervised learning in general, the reader is referred to Chapelle *et al.* (2006b) or Zhu (2008). In order to learn from just a few labeled data points, the models have to make strong assumptions about the data. One can categorize semi-supervised classification methods according to such assumptions. Historically, the first semi-supervised algorithms were based on the idea that, if two points belong to the same cluster, they have the same label. This is called the *cluster* assumption. If this assumption holds, it is reasonable to expect that the optimal decision boundary should stay in a *low density region*. Methods which fall into this category are the transductive SVMs (Joachims, 1999) and the information regularization framework (Szummer & Jaakkola, 2002). The TSVM works by maximizing the margin on the unlabeled data. More concretely, be L the set of labeled instances and U the set of unlabeled ones, while a SVM solves a problem like

$$\min_{\Theta} \sum_{i \in L} \max(0, 1 - y_i \hat{y}_i(\Theta)) + \lambda_1 ||\Theta||^2$$

where Θ are model parameters. The TSVM adds another term that assures that the margin is also maximum on the unlabeled datapoints:

$$\min_{\hat{y}} \sum_{i \in L} \max(0, 1 - y_i \hat{y}_i(\Theta)) + \lambda_1 ||\Theta||^2 + \lambda_2 \sum_{i \in U} \max(0, 1 - |\hat{y}_i(\Theta)|) \, .$$

The information regularization framework operates in a similar way but in a probabilistic framework. This framework adds a regularization term that penalizes changes in the labels in high density areas. As pointed out by Zhu (2008), the low density assumption does not hold true if, for instance, the data is generated by two highly overlapping gaussians. In this case, a *generative model* like the EM with mixture models (Nigam *et al.*, 2006) would be able to devise an appropriate classifier.

The second most relevant assumption is that data points lie on a low dimensional manifold Belkin & Niyogi (2004) and that points that are close to each other in the manifold should have similar labels. Methods based on this assumption use dimensionality reduction techniques to avoid the curse of dimensionality. One can think of the *manifold* assumption as the cluster assumption on the manifold. A successful approach implementing this assumption is the class of algorithms based on manifold regularization (Belkin *et al.*, 2006; Melacci & Belkin, 2011), which regularizes the model by forcing points with short geodesic distances, i.e. distances over the manifold surface, to have similar values for the decision function. Since the geodesic distances are computed based on the Laplacian of a graph representation of the data, these methods can also be regarded as graph-based methods. This class of semi-supervised algorithms, like the Spectral Graph Transducer (Joachims, 2003), define a graph where the nodes are the data points and the edge weights are the similarity between them. Then a loss function is defined, usually regularizing the model so that neighbor nodes are more likely to have the same label. Traditionally, graph based methods rely on the Laplacian of the similarity graph to achieve this. Be $\hat{\mathbf{y}}$ a vector containing the predictions for both labeled and unlabeled datapoints, the Laplacian regularization term can be written as:

$$\frac{1}{(|L| + |U|)^2}\hat{\mathbf{y}}^\top \Delta \hat{\mathbf{y}}$$

where $\Delta = \mathbf{D} - \mathbf{W}$ is the Laplacian of the data adjacency graph, $\mathbf{W}$ is the matrix containing its edge weights and $\mathbf{D}$ is a diagonal matrix where $d_{ii} = \sum_{j \in L \cup U} w_{ij}$. For instance, the Laplacian SVM (LapSVM) and Laplacian regularized least squares (LapRLS) (Belkin *et al.*, 2006; Melacci & Belkin, 2011) use this regularization term.

A number of models can be seen as special cases of this framework. The methods based on Gaussian Fields and Harmonic functions (Zhu *et al.*, 2003) for instance also use a regularizer term based on the graph Laplacian given by $\hat{\mathbf{y}}^\top \Delta \hat{\mathbf{y}}$. The local and global consistency method (Zhou *et al.*, 2004) optimizes the squared loss plus the regularization term from above, but uses instead of Δ the normalized Laplacian $\mathbf{D}^{-\frac{1}{2}}\Delta\mathbf{D}^{-\frac{1}{2}}$. These methods can be seen as special cases of the manifold regularization framework (Belkin *et al.*, 2006) which allows for different loss functions to be plugged in and the graph-based regularizer can work with both the graph Laplacian and its normalized variant.

All of those methods have been shown to be effective when their underlying assumptions hold true. However, when this is not the case, their performance might actually be worsened by unlabeled data (Cozman *et al.*, 2003). The factorization models proposed here are more flexible regarding the structure of the data. They do not require the decision function to lie in a low density region, but instead map the features to a space where they are easily separable. Furthermore, these methods do not assume that the data points lie in a lower dimensional space (although they profit from that when true), since the number of latent features used may be arbitrarily large. Finally, while graph based methods exploit the relative distances between points by a regularizing term based on the Laplacian of the similarity graph, our model does it by factorizing the nearest neighbor matrix. The contribution of such matrix to the model can be adjusted so that the model is robust to datasets where this information is not relevant.

5.2.2 Multi-Relational Factorization for Semi-Supervised Classification

Factorization models have been traditionally used in standard machine learning tasks as dimensionality reduction techniques, where once the latent features are learned, they are fed into a standard classifier. A distinction between such approaches is whether they are (i) *unsupervised* (Tang & Liu, 2009a), which means that they do not use information about the target variables and just factorize the predictors matrix instead, or (ii) *supervised* (Menon & Elkan, 2010; Zhu *et al.*, 2007) which means that they exploit information about the target variables when learning the latent features. A supervised factorization approach for classification like the one from Menon & Elkan (2010) can be seen as a CMF model (Singh & Gordon, 2008b) applied to a dataset comprising the predictors matrix and the matrix containing the target variables.

Multi-matrix factorization as predictive models have been investigated by Zhu *et al.* (2007) and Singh & Gordon (2008b). Here we are interested in how the factorization models themselves work as classifiers, more specifically in a semi-supervised scenario. This means that, besides exploiting the information on the target variable we also exploit the information about unlabeled instances. Semi-supervised classification can be cast as a factorization problem. Previous work on the semi-supervised learning of factorization models has either focused on different tasks or had different goals from this work. Wang *et al.* (2008) use the label information to regularize a factorization model for clustering, meaning that they use label information to improve the performance on an unsupervised learning task, i.e. clustering. Here, however, we are interested in learning predictive models of these labels and investigating how unlabeled data can help to improve the predictive performance of supervised models. Weinberger *et al.* (2005) build on semi-supervised manifold learning techniques to propose a kernel matrix factorization method for non-linear dimensionality reduction. While we do exploit dimensionality reduction, our main goal here is to predict labels of test instances, while Weinberger *et al.* (2005) focus on the task of learning the lower dimensional embedding of the data. Liu *et al.* (2006) propose a semi-supervised learning method for multi-label learning based on non-negative matrix factorization. Their method relies on ad-hoc similarity measures for instances and class labels that should be chosen for each kind of data. Moreover their method only works for multi-label cases whereas the approach presented here deals with binary classification.

Finally, the factorization models can also exploit neighborhood information through manifold regularization as in the clustering method proposed by Cai *et al.* (2008), where the authors propose to use $\mathbf{W}$ as the adjacency matrix of the nearest neighbor graph and regularize a standard unsupervised non-negative matrix factorization model with the Laplacian regularization based on $\mathbf{W}$. Here besides being interest in the semi-supervised classification scenario, instead of adding the Laplacian regularization term, we factorize the nearest neighbor matrix collectively with the predictor and label matrices.

5.3 Semi-supervised classification problem formulation

In order to solve classification problems using multi-factorization models, one first needs to formulate them using a multi-relational framework. A traditional supervised learning problem can be represented in a relational setting with three entity types $\mathcal{E} := \{I, F, T\}$, namely data instances I, features F and target variables T. Data are represented by a predictors matrix $\mathbf{X} \in \mathbb{R}^{|I| \times |F|}$, where each row represents an instance predictor vector $\mathbf{x_i} \in \mathbb{R}^{|F|}$, F being the set of predictors, and a target matrix $\mathbf{Y} \in \mathbb{R}^{|I| \times |T|}$, with each row $\mathbf{y_i}$ containing the values of the target variables for the instance i. These two matrices are represented as the two relations in the multi-relational setting, namely X and Y. Relation X can be defined as

$$X \subseteq I \times F \times \mathbb{R}$$

such that for a given observation $(i, f, x_{if}) \in X$, x_{if} corresponds to the value on the i-th row and f-th column of the predictors matrix $\mathbf{X}$.

Depending on the task, $\mathbf{Y}$ can take various forms. For instance, in a classical binary classification problem, $\mathbf{Y}$ is a one dimensional matrix (i.e. a vector) $\mathbf{y} \in \{-1, +1\}^{|I|}$, while in a regression task it is a real valued vector $\mathbf{y} \in \mathbb{R}^{|I|}$ and in a multi-label classification problem it takes the form of a matrix $\mathbf{Y} \in \{-1, +1\}^{|I| \times |T|}$, T being the set of target variables. Throughout this chapter, the binary classification setting will be considered with only one target variable. Thus the target relation Y is defined as

$$Y \subseteq I \times T \times \{-1, +1\}$$

and each observation $(i, t, y_{it}) \in Y$ corresponds to an element of the matrix $\mathbf{Y}$.

Generally speaking, a learning algorithm learns a model from some training data $D^{\text{train}} := (X^{\text{train}}, Y^{\text{train}})$ that is able to predict the values in some test data Y^{test} given X^{test}, all unseen when learning.

In the semi-supervised learning scenario, there are two distinct sets of training instances: the first comes with their respective labels, i.e. X_L^{train} and Y_L^{train}; the second is composed of training instances for which their respective labels are not known during training time, i.e. X_U^{train}, thus the training data is composed by $D^{\text{train}} := (X_L^{\text{train}}, X_U^{\text{train}}, Y_L^{\text{train}})$. This means that no observations on the target relation Y^{train} are available for instances appearing in X_U^{train}.

At this point, learning problems can again be separated into two different settings. In some situations, it is known during the learning time which instances should have their labels predicted. This is called *transductive* learning (Gammerman *et al.*, 1998). In other situations however, the focus is on learning a general model able to make predictions based on instances unknown during learning, which is called the *inductive* setting. Table 5.1 summarizes the different learning settings discussed here. In this work, we focus on the transductive semi-supervised setting.

Table 5.1: **Different set ups for machine learning problems with labeled data**

		D^{train}	D^{test}
Inductive	Supervised	$X^{\text{train}}, Y^{\text{train}}$	$X^{\text{test}}, Y^{\text{test}}$
	Semi-Supervised	$X_L^{\text{train}}, X_U^{\text{train}}, Y_L^{\text{train}}$	$X^{\text{test}}, Y^{\text{test}}$
Transductive		$X^{\text{train}}, X^{\text{test}}, Y^{\text{train}}$	Y^{test}

5.4 Factorization models for Semi-supervised Classification

In a classification problem the predictor matrix $\mathbf{X}$ and their respective targets $\mathbf{y}$ are given. Each instance $i \in I$, feature $f \in F$ and target variable $t \in T$ are mapped to latent factors through mappings

$$\varphi : I \cup F \cup T \to \mathbb{R}^k$$

where k is the number of latent features used. This way, $\varphi(i)$ is a k-dimensional representation of instance i. With a slight abuse of notation, we will use $\varphi(I) \in \mathbb{R}^{|I| \times k}$ to denote the matrix formed by stacking the vectors $\varphi(i)$. Be $I = \{i_1, \ldots, i_{|I|}\}$, then

$$\varphi(I) := \begin{bmatrix} \varphi(i_1) \\ \vdots \\ \varphi(i_{|I|}) \end{bmatrix}.$$

The matrices $\varphi(F)$ and $\varphi(T)$ are analogously defined to be the formed by stacking the feature vectors of the elements in F and T respectively. Since we are dealing with a binary classification problem, there is only one target variable t, i.e. $|T| = 1$ and $\mathcal{Y}_T = \{-1, +1\}$. Since in this problem there is only one target relation, and there are no signature clash problems we will use a simple collective factorization model like the one by Singh & Gordon (2008b). The model for the relation X is a function of the latent features of instances and predictors $\varphi(I), \varphi(F)$, i.e.

$$x_{if} \approx \hat{x}(\varphi(i), \varphi(f)) = \hat{x}_{if}$$

and for the target relation Y as a function of $\varphi(T)$ and $\varphi(I)$, i.e.

$$y_{it} \approx \hat{y}(\varphi(i), \varphi(t)) = \hat{y}_{it} .$$

For the purposes of this chapter, the approximation functions will be the product of the latent feature vectors, i.e.:

$$\hat{x}_{if} := \varphi(i)^\top \varphi(f)$$
$$\hat{y}_{it} := \varphi(i)^\top \varphi(t)$$

This task can be defined as finding the latent feature matrices $\varphi(I), \varphi(F), \varphi(T)$, that optimize a specific case of Equation 2.9, as in Equation 5.1.

$$J(\varphi(I), \varphi(F), \varphi(T)) := \alpha \sum_{(i,f,x_{if}) \in D_X^{\text{train}}} l_X(x_{if}, \varphi(i)^\top \varphi(f))$$
$$+ (1 - \alpha) \sum_{(i,t,y_{it}) \in D_Y^{\text{train}}} l_Y(y_{it}, \varphi(i)^\top \varphi(t))$$
$$+ Reg(\varphi(I), \varphi(F), \varphi(T)) \tag{5.1}$$

This model allows for different possible choices for l_X and l_Y. Since it is common to represent instances of a classification problem as real valued feature vectors (and this is the case for the datasets used in our experiments), we used the squared loss as l_X. For l_Y, a number of losses are suited for classification problems. We use the hinge loss here, since we are dealing with binary classification problems. In principle, any loss function can be used, so the one that best fits the task at hand should be selected.

One drawback of using the hinge loss is that it is not smooth, meaning that it is not straightforward to optimize it using standard gradient-based methods. To circumvent this, we use the smooth hinge loss proposed by Rennie (2005):

$$h(y, \hat{y}) := \begin{cases} \frac{1}{2} - y\hat{y} & \text{if } y\hat{y} \leq 0, \\ \frac{1}{2}(1 - y\hat{y})^2 & \text{if } 0 < y\hat{y} < 1, \\ 0 & \text{if } y\hat{y} \geq 1 \end{cases} \tag{5.2}$$

5.4.1 Neighborhood Based Feature Extraction

The model presented so far is flexible enough for fitting a variety of datasets, but it still can not handle non linear decision boundaries unless a very high number of latent dimensions is used, which are difficult to estimate from few labeled data. On the top of that, if the data follow the manifold assumption (i.e. data points lying next to each other on the manifold tend to have the same labels), the factorization model presented so far, will not be able to exploit this fact to learn better decision boundaries. Because we use a linear prediction model for Y, if the data is not linearly separable in the learned latent space, the algorithm will fail to find a good decision boundary. This problem can be circumvented by forcing that the nearest-neighborhood relationship is maintained on the latent space. This works because the factorization of Y forces the labeled points from different classes to be further apart from each other in the latent space. Forcing that the neighborhood in the original space is preserved in the latent space will make the unlabeled points to be "dragged" towards their nearest labeled neighbor, thus separating clusters or structures in the data, making it easier to find a good decision boundary that is linear in the latent space (see the Two Moons example in Figure 5.1).

To accomplish this, a new relation is added to the problem, namely a neighborhood relationship. This way, the latent representations are forced to reconstruct the neighborhood relationships thus preserving them in the learned latent space. First a p-nearest neighbor graph is constructed and represented by its adjacency matrix $\mathbf{N} \in \mathbb{R}^{|I| \times |I|}$, where each position n_{ij} is 1 if instance j is one of the p nearest neighbors of i and 0 otherwise. The relation N is then defined as

$$N \subseteq I \times I \times \{0, 1\}$$

and the prediction function for N as

$$\hat{n}_{ij} := \varphi(i)^\top \varphi(j)$$

This enforces instances close to each other to have similar latent features, thus being close in the latent space. We call this model the *Predictor/Neighborhood/Target Collective Matrix Factorization (PNT-CMF)*. Complexity control is achieved using Tikhonov regularization. The objective function we optimize PNT-CMF for in this chapter is shown in Equation 5.3, where $|| \cdot ||_F$ stands for the Frobenius norm.

$$
\begin{aligned}
J(\varphi(I), \varphi(F), \varphi(T)) := {} & \alpha_X \sum_{(i,f,x_{if}) \in D_X^{\text{train}}} (x_{if} - \varphi(i)^\top \varphi(f))^2 \\
& + \alpha_N \sum_{(i,j,n_{ij}) \in D_N^{\text{train}}} (n_{ij} - \varphi(i)^\top \varphi(j))^2 \\
& + \alpha_Y \sum_{(i,t,y_{it}) \in D_Y^{\text{train}}} h(y_{it}, \varphi(i)^\top \varphi(t)) \\
& + \lambda_I ||\varphi(I)||_F^2 + \lambda_F ||\varphi(F)||_F^2 + \lambda_T ||\varphi(T)||_F^2
\end{aligned}
\tag{5.3}
$$

The hyperparameter α_N controls the importance of the nearest neighbor relation to the model. This is a very important parameter since that, if the data does not have a cluster structure, or if it has a misleading cluster structure (i.e. points belonging to different classes in the same cluster), the factorization of N will harm the model more than help to improve its performance.

It is important to point out that factorizing the nearest neighbor matrix is related to, but differs from, the concept of manifold regularization (Belkin *et al.*, 2006). Manifold regularization forces instances close to each other to have similar values in the decision function. Forcing that neighbors have similar latent features causes the same effect in the PNT-CMF multi-matrix factorization model. It has been observed however that, if the data does not follow the manifold or cluster assumption, manifold regularization based methods like Laplacian SVM and Laplacian Regularized Least Squares fail to find a good solution (Chapelle *et al.*, 2006a). In this case the best solution is to set the Laplacian regularization constant to zero, reducing the model to a fully supervised one, not taking advantage of the unlabeled data points. Here, by setting $\alpha_N = 0$ one still has a powerful semi-supervised model that simply does not rely on the neighborhood relation. The experiments conducted in this chapter provide some empirical evidence that it is possible to automatically estimate good values for α_N without any background knowledge on the dataset through model selection, although further investigation in this direction is needed.

5.4.2 Semi-Supervised Learning of PNT-CMF

In a transductive setting, the test instances predictors are available at training time. A factorization model can naturally make use of this information by adding those predictors to the X matrix. If Y is only partially observed, then the training data for the transductive factorization model is

$$X := \begin{bmatrix} X^{\text{train}} \\ X^{\text{test}} \end{bmatrix}, Y := \begin{bmatrix} Y^{\text{train}} \\ ? \end{bmatrix}$$

Here non-observed values are denoted by a question mark. Learning a transductive model means optimizing a factorization model for Equation 5.3 on the data above.

There are a few choices about how to learn PNT-CMF. Here we favor the all-at-once approach similar to what is done by Singh & Gordon (2008b) since on the one hand it has been shown to yield better results (Krohn-Grimberghe *et al.*, 2012) and, on the other hand, the learning of the Y factorization profits more from it.

Algorithm 5 Stochastic gradient descent algorithm for learning PNT-CMF

1: **procedure** LEARNPNT-CMF
    input: $D^{\mathrm{train}}, \lambda_I, \lambda_F, \lambda_T, \alpha_X, \alpha_Y, \alpha_K, k, p, \eta$
    output: $\varphi(I), \varphi(F), \varphi(T)$

2:    `/* I denotes the k x k identity matrix */`
3:    $\varphi(I) \sim \mathcal{N}(0, \sigma\mathbf{I})$
4:    $\varphi(F) \sim \mathcal{N}(0, \sigma\mathbf{I})$
5:    $\varphi(T) \sim \mathcal{N}(0, \sigma\mathbf{I})$
6:    $N \leftarrow \mathrm{computeNearestNeighborMatrix}(X, p)$
7:    **repeat**
8:        draw uniformly $(i, f, x_{if}) \sim D_X^{\mathrm{train}}$
9:        $\varphi(i) \leftarrow \varphi(i) - \eta \left(\alpha_X \frac{\partial}{\partial\varphi(i)} l_X(x_{if}, \varphi(i)^\top\varphi(f)) + \lambda_I\varphi(i) \right)$
10:      $\varphi(f) \leftarrow \varphi(f) - \eta \left(\alpha_X \frac{\partial}{\partial\varphi(f)} l_X(x_{if}, \varphi(i)^\top\varphi(f)) + \lambda_F\varphi(f) \right)$
11:      draw uniformly $(i, j, n_{ij}) \sim D_N$
12:      $\varphi(i) \leftarrow \varphi(i) - \eta \left(\alpha_N \frac{\partial}{\partial\varphi(i)} l_N(n_{ij}, \varphi(i)^\top\varphi(j)) + \lambda_I\varphi(i) \right)$
13:      $\varphi(j) \leftarrow \varphi(j) - \eta \left(\alpha_N \frac{\partial}{\partial\varphi(j)} l_N(n_{ij}, \varphi(i)^\top\varphi(j)) + \lambda_I\varphi(j) \right)$
14:      draw uniformly $(i, t, y_{it}) \sim D_Y^{\mathrm{train}}$
15:      $\varphi(i) \leftarrow \varphi(i) - \eta \left(\alpha_y \frac{\partial}{\partial\varphi(i)} l_Y(y_{it}, \varphi(i)^\top\varphi(t)) + \lambda_I\varphi(i) \right)$
16:      $\varphi(t) \leftarrow \varphi(t) - \eta \left(\alpha_y \frac{\partial}{\partial\varphi(t)} l_Y(y_{it}, \varphi(i)^\top\varphi(t)) + \lambda_T\varphi(t) \right)$
17:    **until** convergence
18:    **return** $\varphi(I), \varphi(F), \varphi(T)$
19: **end procedure**

To learn this model, a stochastic gradient descent algorithm is applied as shown in Algorithm 5. The algorithm starts by randomly initializing the parameters to be learned. The values for each one of them are drawn from a normal distribution with mean 0 and variance 0.001. Following this, the neighborhood is computed based on a distance measure d. In this chapter we used the euclidean distance $d(\mathbf{x}_i, \mathbf{x}_j) := ||\mathbf{x}_i - \mathbf{x}_j||^2$. Next, the parameters are updated in the direction of the negative gradient of each loss scaled by a learn rate η. Since l_X is defined to be the squared loss, its derivatives are

$$\frac{\partial}{\partial\varphi(i)} l_X(x_{if}, \varphi(i)^\top\varphi(f)) := -2(x_{if} - \varphi(i)^\top\varphi(f))\varphi(f)$$

$$\frac{\partial}{\partial\varphi(f)}l_X(x_{if},\varphi(i)^\top\varphi(f)) := -2(x_{if} - \varphi(i)^\top\varphi(f))\varphi(i)$$

Analog to that, the l_K derivatives are

$$\frac{\partial}{\partial\varphi(i)}l_N(n_{ij},\varphi(i)^\top\varphi(j)) := -2(n_{ij} - \varphi(i)^\top\varphi(j))\varphi(j)$$

$$\frac{\partial}{\partial\varphi(j)}l_N(n_{ij},\varphi(i)^\top\varphi(j)) := -2(n_{ij} - \varphi(i)^\top\varphi(j))\varphi(i)$$

Be $z_{it} := y_{it} \cdot \varphi(i)^\top\varphi(t)$, the loss function l_Y has the following partial derivatives:

$$\frac{\partial}{\partial\varphi(i)}l_Y(y_{it},\varphi(i)^\top\varphi(t)) := \frac{dh(z_{it})}{dz_{it}}y_{it}\varphi(t)$$

$$\frac{\partial}{\partial\varphi(t)}l_Y(y_{it},\varphi(i)^\top\varphi(t)) := \frac{dh(z_{it})}{dz_{it}}y_{it}\varphi(i)$$

where:

$$\frac{dh(z)}{dz} = \begin{cases} -1 & \text{if } z \leq 0, \\ z - 1 & \text{if } 0 < z < 1, \\ 0 & \text{if } z \geq 1 \end{cases}$$

5.4.3 Learning Inductive Factorization models for Classification

The same model could be used in an inductive setting, where the instances for which we want to make predictions are not known during training time. This can be achieved by using as training data for relation X only the information of the predictors of labeled instances. In this process, the training data for the inductive model is

$$X := X^{\text{train}}, Y := Y^{\text{train}}$$

One drawback of this approach is that, in order to make out-of-sample predictions, the latent representations of the test instances need to be inferred for each test instance separately. In relational learning terms, this means that it is desired to make predictions for instances never seen during the training process. In other words, for a previously unseen instance $u \in I$, its respective latent feature vector $\varphi(u)$ is not computed during the training phase. We approach this problem by

---

Algorithm 6 Mapping a new observation to the same latent space of a previously learned PNT-CMF model. This is used for making out-of-sample predictions

---

1: **procedure** FOLDIN-INSTANCE
    input: $X^{(u)}, u, \varphi(I), \varphi(F), \lambda_I, \alpha_X, \alpha_N, d, p, \eta$
    output: $\varphi(u)$

2:     $\varphi(u) \sim \mathcal{N}(0, \sigma\mathbf{I})$
3:     $N^{(u)} \leftarrow \text{computeNearestNeighborVector}(x_i, X, d, p)$
4:     **repeat**
5:         draw uniformly $(u, f, x_{uf}) \sim X^{(u)}$
6:         $\varphi(u) \leftarrow \varphi(u) - \eta\left(\alpha_X \frac{\partial}{\partial\varphi(u)} l_X(x_{uf}, \varphi(i)^\top\varphi(f)) + \lambda_I\varphi(u)\right)$
7:         draw uniformly $(u, j, n_{uj}) \sim N^{(u)}$
8:         $\varphi(u) \leftarrow \varphi(u) - \eta\left(\alpha_N \frac{\partial}{\partial\varphi(u)} l_N(n_{uj}, \varphi(i)^\top\varphi(j)) + \lambda_I\varphi(u)\right)$
9:     **until** convergence
10:    **return** $\varphi(u)$
11: **end procedure**

---

adding a fold-inFold-in step after learning the model. The fold-in step takes a new instance u and maps it to the same latent feature space as the training instances. One straight-forward way to accomplish this is to minimize Equation 5.4. This is done by Algorithm 6. In the algorithm, $X^{(u)}$ denotes the the observations about u on relation X, i.e., its predictors. More formally:

$$X^{(u)} := \{(u, f, x_{uf}) | (u, f, x_{uf}) \in X\}$$

$$\min_{\varphi(u)} J(u, \varphi(u), \varphi(I), \varphi(F)) := \alpha_X \sum_{f \in F}(x_{uf} - \varphi(u)^\top\varphi(f))^2$$

$$+ \alpha_N \sum_{j \in I}(n_{uj} - \varphi(u)^\top\varphi(j))^2 + \lambda_I||\varphi(u)||^2 \quad (5.4)$$

5.5   Evaluation

The main goals of the experiments are: (i) compare PNT-CMF against state-of-the-art semi-supervised classifiers; (ii) assess the robustness and competitiveness

Table 5.2: **Dataset characteristics**

Dataset	# Instances	# Predictors
g241c	1500	241
g241d	1500	241
digit	1500	241
bci	400	117
usps	1500	241
text	1500	11960

of our factorization model across datasets with different characteristics; 3.) observe how useful semi-supervised transductive factorization models are compared to their inductive supervised counterparts (i.e. we want to observe how much can factorization models benefit from unlabeled data).

5.5.1 Datasets

Chapelle *et al.* (2006a) have run an extensive benchmark analysis of semi-supervised learning models on 6 datasets, which are also used here. A summary of the data used in the experiments can be found in Table 5.2. The task for all data sets is binary classification. Here we note that we conduct experiments only on binary classification in order to not contaminate the results with influences from different tasks. The application and evaluation of the model on other tasks like multi-class and multi-label classification and regression is left for future work.

5.5.2 Setup

For the evaluation of the methods proposed here, we employed the same protocol used in the benchmark analysis presented by Chapelle *et al.* (2006a), which is standard in the evaluation of semi-supervised classifiers. Each dataset, comes with two different sets of splits: the first one with 10 randomly chosen labeled training instances and the second with 100, each one with 12 splits. The exactly same splits used by Chapelle *et al.* (2006a) were employed her and they are available for download[1]. Each model was evaluated on a transductive semi-supervised setting. In order to be able to answer to question 3 posed in the beginning of this section, we also evaluated the models on a fully supervised setting.

---

[1] http://olivier.chapelle.cc/ssl-book/benchmarks.html

The performance of the model was measured using the hinge loss. Hinge loss is used since it is the measure the evaluated models are optimized for. The hinge loss is defined per target variable. Since in these experiments there is only one target variable, i.e. $|T| = 1$, the hinge loss of a variable t is defined in Equation 5.5. It is worth noting that the *lower* the hinge loss the *better*.

$$\text{hinge}(Y^{\text{test}}, \hat{y}, t) := \frac{1}{|Y^{\text{test}}|} \sum_{(i,t,y_{it}) \in Y^{\text{test}}} \max(0, 1 - (y_{it} \cdot \hat{y}_{it})) \tag{5.5}$$

The AUC a target variable t is also considered, as it is a widely used classification evaluation measure. Be

$$\mathcal{I}^{\text{test}}_{t,+} := \{i | (i, t, +1) \in Y^{\text{test}}\}$$

the set of positive instances and

$$\mathcal{I}^{\text{test}}_{t,-} := \{i | (i, t, -1) \in Y^{\text{test}}\}$$

the set of negative ones and $\delta(b)$ the indicator function which is 1 if b is true and 0 otherwise, the AUC of a binary classifier is defined in Equation 5.6. The *higher* the AUC score of a model, the *better*.

$$\text{AUC}(Y^{\text{test}}, \hat{y}, t) := \frac{1}{|\mathcal{I}^{\text{test}}_{t,+}||\mathcal{I}^{\text{test}}_{t,-}|} \sum_{i \in \mathcal{I}^{\text{test}}_{t,+}} \sum_{j \in \mathcal{I}^{\text{test}}_{t,-}} \delta(\hat{y}_{it} > \hat{y}_{jt}) \tag{5.6}$$

5.5.3 Baselines

We compare PNT-CMF against representative methods implementing the two most important assumptions of semi-supervised learning. As a representative of the manifold assumption we chose the Laplacian SVM (LapSVM) trained in the primal (Melacci & Belkin, 2011), since manifold regularization has been one of the most successful approaches for semi-supervised learning.

The second baseline is the transductive version of SVMs (TSVM) (Joachims, 1999) which implements the low density (or cluster) assumption. On the inductive case, TSVM reduces to a standard SVM.

Besides being representatives of their working assumptions, both LapSVM and TSVM optimize the same loss used for PNT-CMF in this chapter. Other graph based methods like local and global consistency (Zhou *et al.*, 2004) and the one based on Gaussian Fields and Harmonic functions (Zhu *et al.*, 2003) work under the same assumptions of LapSVM using a similar mathematical machinery (as discussed in section 5.2.1) but optimize the squared loss instead. By having all the competitor methods optimizing the same loss, the effects observed come from the models only and not from the usage of different losses.

At last, since PNT-CMF performs dimensionality reduction and LapSVM operates on a lower dimensional manifold, we add a fourth competitor method which incorporates dimensionality reduction to TSVM as well: we applied PCA dimensionality reduction to all datasets and ran TSVM using the transformed data. This method is called PCA+TSVM. For each dataset we used the first k PCA dimensions, k being the same number of latent dimensions used by PNT-CMF.

As a TSVM implementation we used *SVMLight*[1]. For LapSVM we used the implementation from Melacci & Belkin (2011), which is also available for download[2].

5.5.4 Model Selection

Model selection is a known problem for semi-supervised learning due to the low number of labeled instances available. We show that it is possible to estimate good hyperparameters for PNT-CMF even in the presence of only a few labeled data points. For **PNT-CMF**, each hyperparameter combination was evaluated through 5-fold cross-validation using **only the training data.**

We gave the **baseline methods** a competitive advantage: we estimated their hyperparameters using **both train and test data.** Each baseline model was learned on the training data using different hyperparameter combinations from a fine grained grid and then evaluated on the respective test data. The combination that delivered the best scores **on test** was chosen, thus producing an upper bound of their performance. We also observe that the results for the competitor methods are consistent with the ones reported in the literature for the same datasets.

5.5.5 Results and discussion

The hinge loss scores for the datasets with 10 and 100 labeled examples are shown in Figure 5.2. For each method and dataset, the average performance over the 12 splits is shown. The error bars represent the 99% confidence intervals.

---

[1] http://svmlight.joachims.org/
[2] http://www.dii.unisi.it/~melacci/lapsvmp/

Table 5.3: **Summary of the statistically significant winners for the transductive setting on the Hinge Loss. Cells in boldface indicate that PNT-CMF is the winner alone. Italic ones indicate a tie with PNT-CMF among the winners.**

		Hinge Loss	
		10 labeled	100 labeled
Manifold	digit	**PNT-CMF**	**PNT-CMF**
	usps	**PNT-CMF**	**PNT-CMF**
	bci	*PNT-CMF, LapSVM*	*PNT-CMF, LapSVM, PCASVM*
Cluster	g241c	**PNT-CMF**	**PNT-CMF**
	g241d	**PNT-CMF**	**PNT-CMF**
	text	*PNT-CMF, TSVM*	TSVM

Chapelle *et al.* (2006a) divide these datasets into two categories: the **manifold-like** and the **cluster-like**. The **manifold** group comprises the *digit, usps* and *bci* datasets in which the data lie near a low dimensional manifold. Algorithms like LapSVM are expected to excel in these datasets. *g241c, g241d* and *text* fall under the category of **cluster-like** datasets in which different classes do not share the same cluster thus making the optimal decision boundary to lie in a low density region, favoring algorithms like TSVM.

The left-hand side of Figure 5.2 show how PNT-CMF performs in comparison to its competitors. By looking especially at this figure, one can see that TSVM is stronger in the *g241c* and *text* datasets while LapSVM is more competitive in the manifold-like data. One can also see that LapSVM is significantly weaker on the *g241c* and *text* sets where the data do not lie near a low dimensional manifold. PNT-CMF on the other hand is always either the statistically significant winner or is away from the winner by a non significant margin. The best performers on each dataset can be found on tables 5.3 and 5.4. Out of the 12 experiments, PNT-CMF is the sole winner in 8 of them and is one of the winning methods in all the 3 ties, with TSVM winning in one case, and only for 100 labeled instances. This supports our claim that PNT-CMF can consistently work well under different assumptions. In accordance with our expectations, LapSVM pops up more often on the upper part of the table corresponding to the manifold-like datasets while TSVM always appears on the cluster-like datasets.

The results for AUC are shown in Figure 5.3. As for the hinge loss figures, the average performance over the 12 splits is shown and the error bars represent the 99% confidence intervals. Although the distances between the methods are

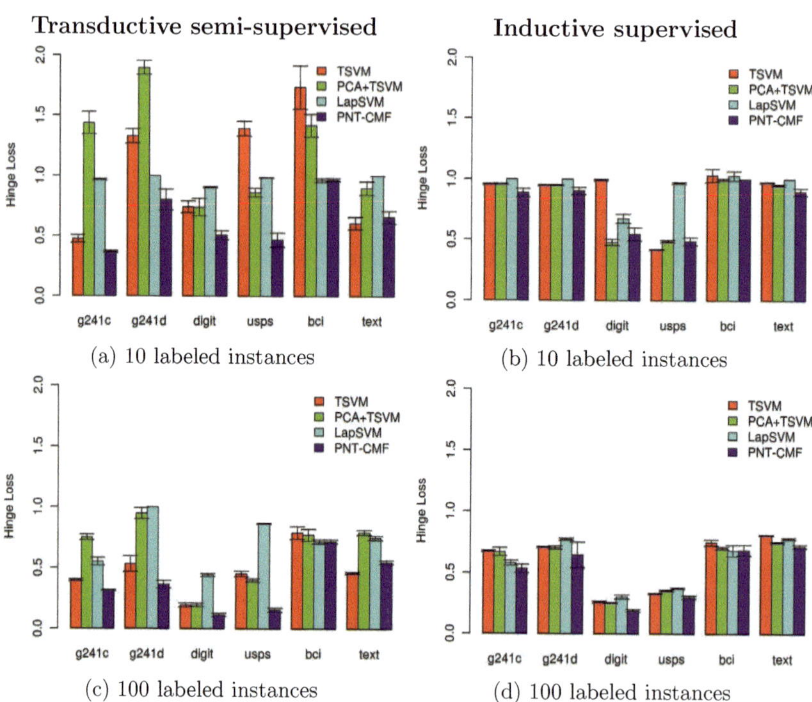

(a) 10 labeled instances

(b) 10 labeled instances

(c) 100 labeled instances

(d) 100 labeled instances

Figure 5.2: Results for the Hinge Loss. The *lower* the better.

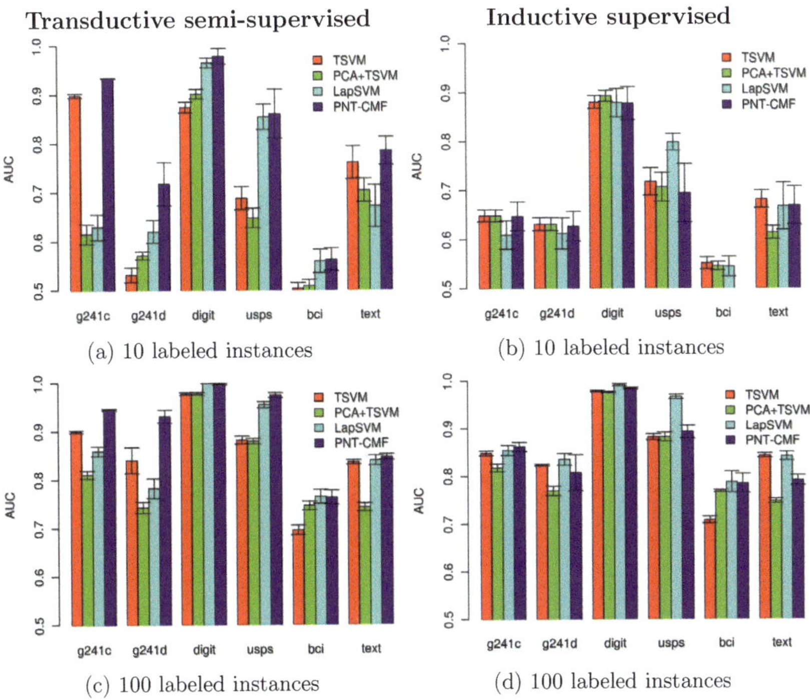

(a) 10 labeled instances

(b) 10 labeled instances

(c) 100 labeled instances

(d) 100 labeled instances

Figure 5.3: Results for AUC. The *higher* the better

smaller regarding AUC, the trends are the same as for the hinge loss. Table 5.4 shows the statistically significant winners for AUC on each dataset. Out of the 12 experiments, PNT-CMF is the sole winner in 5 of them and is one of the winning methods in all the 7 ties.

Combining the figures from tables 5.3 and 5.4, there are a total of 24 experiments in which PNT-CMF is the sole winner in 13 of them and is one of the winning methods in all the 10 ties, with TSVM winning in one case.

Finally, by comparing the right and left hand sides of Figure 5.2 and Figure 5.3, we can have an idea of the effects of taking unlabeled data into account. One can observe that TSVM seems to be more unstable, having sometimes worse hinge loss on the semi-supervised case than the corresponding ones on the supervised scenarios for the *bci*, *usps* and *g241d* datasets. The same happens for LapSVM on

Table 5.4: **Summary of the statistically significant winners for the transductive setting on AUC. Cells in boldface indicate that PNT-CMF is the winner alone. Italic ones indicate a tie with PNT-CMF among the winners.**

		AUC	
		10 labeled	100 labeled
Manifold	digit	*PNT-CMF,LapSVM*	*PNT-CMF,LapSVM*
	usps	*PNT-CMF,LapSVM*	**PNT-CMF**
	bci	*PNT-CMF,LapSVM*	*PNT-CMF,LapSVM*
Cluster	g241c	**PNT-CMF**	**PNT-CMF**
	g241d	**PNT-CMF**	**PNT-CMF**
	text	*PNT-CMF,TSVM*	*PNT-CMF,TSVM,LapSVM*

g241d dataset. PNT-CMF seems to be more robust in this sense, not presenting a significant performance degradation in any case.

5.6 Conclusion

In this chapter it has been shown that multi-relational factorization models can be applied to standard machine learning problems. More specifically, the semi-supervised classification was formalized as an instance of the multi-relational learning problem and PNT-CMF, a factorization model for semi-supervised classification was proposed. It has been shown how to learn such models in a transductive (semi-supervised) and in an inductive (supervised) setting. The performance of such models was evaluated on a number of different synthetic and real-world datasets with varying characteristics. The proposed model relies on the reconstruction of the predictors and the neighborhood matrices in the original feature space to learn latent factors used for classification. The contribution of each of them to the model can be controlled in order to fit different kinds of datasets better.

PNT-CMF represents a step forward in the state-of-the-art of semi-supervised classification because, unlike other semi-supervised methods which face a performance degradation when their model assumptions do not hold, the experimental results showed that PNT-CMF is capable of coping with datasets with different characteristics. One evidence for this is that, in all cases, regardless of whether LapSVM or TSVM were the best models, PNT-CMF was always a strong competitor, being among the winners in the vast majority of the semi-supervised experiments.

Possible future work directions are (i) to investigate better factorization strategies for the matrix K, like different loss and reconstruction functions and (ii) the extension and evaluation of the model on regression, multi-class and multi-label classification tasks.

Chapter 6

Conclusion

Contents

This chapter concludes this thesis with a summary of its contents and a discussion of possible future directions.

6.1 Summary

Learning from multi-relational data is an important task in data mining, especially due to the large quantity of available data with relational information and the wide range of tasks it enables, ranging from social network analysis, recommender systems to protein-interaction and Linked Open Data mining.

In this thesis we proposed a formalization for the multi-relational learning problem and described the state-of-the-art under our notational framework. By having all the models described using the same notation we were able to identify similarities and relations between them like for instance the equivalence between LMF and RESCAL. There we argued why the evaluation protocol widely used in the literature does not properly simulate real world scenarios when dealing with data with only positive observations. We show that, in a positive-only situation, the way negative examples are usually generated might lead to a contamination of the training data with information from the test split and propose a new strategy that simulates real world scenarios more accurately.

We also idenfied open problems not yet fully addressed by the sate-of-the-art that were addressed in this work. The first one is to investigate the effect of optimizing loss functions that directly take into considreation the positive-only scenario. For that, we proposed to optimize multi-relational models for the BPR-Opt optimization criterion, from the item recommendation literature and evaluated it on the LOD mining task.

Next we proposed DMF and CATSMF, two frameworks for learning multi-relational factorization models when there are multiple target relations. State-of-the-art models paramatrize their prediction functions in such a way that they learn parameters that perform on average well on all target relations. DMF in turn learns a different model per target relation such that each each model is optimized for each target relation individually. The problem with DMF is that the number of parameters to be learned grows by a factor equals to the number of target relations in the data. CATSMF makes use of the fact that a lot of parameters learned by DMF are not used for prediction, which are called auxiliary parameters. Instead of learning one set of auxiliary parameters per target relation, CATSMF defines only one set of them and shares them between the different models, thus reducing the amount of parameters to be learned without sacrificing predictive performance.

Finally, we showed that multi-relational factorization models can also be applied to standard machine learning tasks like binary classification. We formulate the problem of semi-supervised classification as an instance of a multi-relational learning problem and devise a factorization based semi-supervised classifier called PNT-CMF. PNT-CMF makes use of both features and neighborhood information about the data points and performs supervised dimensionality reduction in parallel with the learning of the classifier. Experiments on real world datasets show that PNT-CMF is competitive against standard semi-supervised classifiers.

6.2 Discussion

From the work in this thesis we can provide some general guidelines for applying multi-relational factorization models to real world problems. Although there is no single best model that can be said to outperform others in all situations, it is possible to delineate some general guidelines to determine the most suitable model for each problem.

The first step, as in many machine learning areas, is to determine what is the task to be solved. This will dictate which loss function to optimize the the model for. This depends on the target space $\mathcal{Y}_r$ of each relation. Usual tasks are regression $\mathcal{Y}_r = \mathbb{R}$, binary classification $\mathcal{Y}_r = \{-1, +1\}$ and, most commonly, classification where the training data consists only of positive observations. In the latter case it is important to use a *Split and Sample* strategy as described in Chapter 2 when splitting the data to perform model selection.

Second it is important to define the parametrization of the prediction function. Using relation features generally leads to better predictive accuracy, especially when there are relations with signature clash. Using symmetric matrices, especially diagonal matrices as relation features, leads to better runtime performance but can be suboptimal but can also lead to lower predictive performance on assymetric relations. Using full asymetric matrices as done by RESCAL (Nickel *et al.*, 2011) results in better predictions at the cost of more computational time and memory resources. If memory resources are crucial, one can resort to the strategy of MOF-SRP (Jenatton *et al.*, 2012) and represent the relation feature matrices as the outer product of rank one matrices. This comes of course at the cost of more computing time.

Finally if there are multiple target relations, learning the model following the CATSMF strategy is the more appropriate approach. Although learning a model with CATSMF will demand more computatonal resources than learning the same model under a complete sharing strategy, our experiments showed that CATSMF can levearge the performance of models using diagonal matrices as relation features to the level of competitors using full matrices but still demanding less computational resources than RESCAL and MOF-SRP. CATSMF is model independant and can be used to boost the performance of any model.

6.3 Future Direction

Future research directions have been discussed throughout this thesis at the end of each chapter.

The evaluation of the imapct of the loss function presented in Chapter 3 can be extended by investigating what happens when different relations are optimized for different loss functions. State-of-the-art models usually consider that all relations optimize the same type of loss. In Chapter 5 we have an example of a situation where this is not the case. further investigation on this issue and how to properly address it is needed and a possible future research direction.

Another interesting direction for future work is to investigate a more memory efficient CATSMF variant, e.g., by reducing the number of parameters to be learned. One possible alternative to this end would be to introduce an ℓ_1 regularizer so as to remove some of the small parameters and trim the model even further.

Possible future work directions are (i) to investigate better factorization strategies for the matrix K, like different loss and reconstruction functions and (ii) the extension and evaluation of the model on regression, multi-class and multi-label classification tasks.

Index

References

AGARWAL, D., CHEN, B.C. & LONG, B. (2011). Localized Factor Models for Multi-context Recommendation. In *Proceedings of the 17th ACM SIGKDD International Conference on Knowledge Discovery and Data Mining*, KDD '11, 609–617, ACM, New York, NY, USA. 16, 17, 25

BADER, B.W. & KOLDA, T.G. (2006). Algorithm 862: MATLAB tensor classes for fast algorithm prototyping. *ACM Transactions on Mathematical Software*, **32**, 635–653. 42

BELKIN, M. & NIYOGI, P. (2004). Semi-supervised learning on Riemannian manifolds. *Machine Learning*, **56**, 209–239. 81

BELKIN, M., NIYOGI, P. & SINDHWANI, V. (2006). Manifold regularization: A geometric framework for learning from labeled and unlabeled examples. *The Journal of Machine Learning Research*, **7**, 2399–2434. 78, 81, 82, 88

BORDES, A., USUNIER, N., GARCÍA-DURÁN, A., WESTON, J. & YAKHNENKO, O. (2013). Irreflexive and Hierarchical Relations as Translations. *CoRR*, **abs/1304.7158**. 17

BRICKLEY, D. & GUHA, R. (2004). *RDF Vocabulary Description Language 1.0: RDF Schema*. W3C. 30

CAI, D., HE, X., WU, X. & HAN, J. (2008). Non-negative Matrix Factorization on Manifold. In *Proceedings of the 2008 Eighth IEEE International Conference on Data Mining*, ICDM '08, 63–72, IEEE Computer Society, Washington, DC, USA. 83

CARROLL, J.D. & CHANG, J.J. (1970). Analysis of individual differences in multidimensional scaling via an n-way generalization of Eckart-Young decomposition. *Psychometrika*, **35**, 283–319. 28, 29

CHAPELLE, O., SCHÖLKOPF, B. & ZIEN, A. (2006a). Analysis of Benchmarks. In O. Chapelle, B. Schölkopf & A. Zien, eds., *Semi-Supervised Learning*, chap. 21, 377–393, MIT Press, Cambridge, MA. 77, 88, 92, 94

CHAPELLE, O., SCHÖLKOPF, B. & ZIEN, A., eds. (2006b). *Semi-Supervised Learning*. MIT Press, Cambridge, MA. 77, 80

COZMAN, F., COHEN, I. & CIRELO, M. (2003). Semi-supervised learning of mixture models. In *20th International Conference on Machine Learning*, vol. 20, 99–106. 77, 82

CREMONESI, P., KOREN, Y. & TURRIN, R. (2010). Performance of recommender algorithms on top-n recommendation tasks. In *Proceedings of the fourth ACM conference on Recommender systems*, RecSys '10, 39–46, ACM, New York, NY, USA. 23, 64

DECKER, S., BRICKLEY, D., SAARELA, J. & ANGELE, J. (1998). A query and inference service for RDF. In *Online Proceedings of the QL'98 - The Query Languages Workshop*. 28

DENHAM, W.W. (1973). *The Detection of Patterns in Alyawarra Nonverbal Behavior*. Ph.D. thesis, University of Washington. 66

DRUMOND, L., RENDLE, S. & SCHMIDT-THIEME, L. (2012). Predicting RDF triples in incomplete knowledge bases with tensor factorization. In *Proceedings of the 27th Annual ACM Symposium on Applied Computing*, SAC '12, 326–331, ACM, New York, NY, USA. 5, 21, 27, 42, 52

DRUMOND, L., SCHMIDT-THIEME, L., FREUDENTHALER, C. & KROHN-GRIMBERGHE, A. (2014). Collective Matrix Factorization of Predictors, Neighborhood and Targets for Semi-Supervised Classification. In *Proceedings of the The 18th Pacific-Asia Conference on Knowledge Discovery and Data Mining*. 77

ELBASSUONI, S., RAMANATH, M., SCHENKEL, R., SYDOW, M. & WEIKUM, G. (2009). Language-model-based ranking for queries on RDF-graphs. In *Proceeding of the 18th ACM Conference on Information and Knowledge Management*, CIKM '09, 977–986, ACM, New York, NY, USA. 29

ERMIS, B., ACAR, E. & CEMGIL, A.T. (2012). Link Prediction via Generalized Coupled Tensor Factorisation. In *ECML/PKDD Workshop on Collective Learning and Inference on Structured Data*. 19

FRANZ, T., SCHULTZ, A., SIZOV, S. & STAAB, S. (2009). TripleRank: Ranking Semantic Web Data by Tensor Decomposition. In *Proceedings of the 8th International Semantic Web Conference*, ISWC '09, 213–228, Springer-Verlag, Berlin, Heidelberg. 28, 29, 31, 33, 35, 39, 40, 42

FRIEDMAN, N., GETOOR, L., KOLLER, D. & PFEFFER, A. (1999). Learning Probabilistic Relational Models. In *Proceedings of the 16th International Joint Conference on Artificial Intelligence - Volume 2*, IJCAI'99, 1300–1307, Morgan Kaufmann Publishers Inc., San Francisco, CA, USA. 3

GAMMERMAN, A., VOVK, V. & VAPNIK, V. (1998). Learning by Transduction. In *In Proceedings of the Fourteenth Conference on Uncertainty in Artificial Intelligence*, 148–156, Morgan Kaufmann. 84

GETOOR, L. & TASKAR, B., eds. (2007). *Introduction to Statistical Relational Learning*. The MIT Press. 3, 14

GLOROT, X., BORDES, A., WESTON, J. & BENGIO, Y. (2013). A Semantic Matching Energy Function for Learning with Multi-relational Data. *CoRR*, **abs/1301.3485**. 15, 25, 52, 54

HARSHMAN, R. (1970). Foundations of the PARAFAC procedure: Models and conditions for an "explanatory" multi-mode factor. In *UCLA Working Papers in Phonetics*, vol. 16, 1–84. 15

HASTIE, T., TIBSHIRANI, R., FRIEDMAN, J. & CORPORATION, E. (2009). *The Elements of Statistical Learning*. Springer, Dordrecht. 1

HUANG, H. & LIU, C. (2009). Query Evaluation on Probabilistic RDF Databases. In G. Vossen, D. Long & J. Yu, eds., *Web Information Systems Engineering - WISE 2009*, vol. 5802 of *Lecture Notes in Computer Science*, 307–320, Springer. 29

JENATTON, R., ROUX, N.L., BORDES, A. & OBOZINSKI, G. (2012). A latent factor model for highly multi-relational data. Neural Information Processing Systems (NIPS 2012). 4, 5, 15, 16, 22, 24, 25, 35, 52, 54, 63, 67, 69, 70, 71, 102

JOACHIMS, T. (1999). Transductive Inference for Text Classification using Support Vector Machines. In *Proceedings of the 1999 International Conference on Machine Learning (ICML)*. 80, 93

JOACHIMS, T. (2003). Transductive Learning via Spectral Graph Partitioning. In *Proceedings of the International Conference on Machine Learning*, 290–297, AAAI Press. 81

JORGENSEN, B. (1997). *The Theory of Dispersion Models.* Chapman & Hall/CRC Monographs on Statistics & Applied Probability, Taylor & Francis. 19

KARVOUNARAKIS, G., MAGGANARAKI, A., ALEXAKI, S., CHRISTOPHIDES, V., PLEXOUSAKIS, D., SCHOLL, M. & TOLLE, K. (2003). Querying the Semantic Web with RQL. *Comput. Netw.*, **42**, 617–640. 28, 29

KEMP, C., TENENBAUM, J.B., GRIFFITHS, T.L., YAMADA, T. & UEDA, N. (2006). Learning Systems of Concepts with an Infinite Relational Model. In *Proceedings of the 21st National Conference on Artificial Intelligence*, AAAI'06, 381–388, AAAI Press. 3

KERSTING, K. (2006). *An Inductive Logic Programming Approach to Statistical Relational Learning*, vol. 148. Ios PressInc. 3, 14

KLYNE, G. & CARROLL, J. (2004). *Resource Description Framework (RDF): Concepts and Abstract Syntax.* W3C. 30, 34, 35

KOREN, Y., BELL, R. & VOLINSKY, C. (2009). Matrix factorization techniques for recommender systems. *Computer*, **42**, 30–37. 5

KROHN-GRIMBERGHE, A., DRUMOND, L., FREUDENTHALER, C. & SCHMIDT-THIEME, L. (2012). Multi-relational matrix factorization using bayesian personalized ranking for social network data. In *Proceedings of the fifth ACM International Conference on Web Search and Data Mining WSDM '12*, 173–182, ACM, New York, NY, USA. 5, 11, 19, 20, 52, 68, 69, 70, 88

LIPPERT, C., WEBER, S.H., HUANG, Y., TRESP, V., SCHUBERT, M. & KRIEGEL, H.P. (2008). Relation-Prediction in Multi-Relational Domains using Matrix-Factorization. In *NIPS 2008 Workshop: Structured Input - Structured Output.* 5, 11, 15, 25

LIU, Y., JIN, R. & YANG, L. (2006). Semi-supervised multi-label learning by constrained non-negative matrix factorization. In *Proceedings of the National Conference on Artificial Intelligence*, vol. 21, 421, AAAI Press. 83

LONDON, B., REKATSINAS, T., HUANG, B. & GETOOR, L. (2012). Multirelational Weighted Tensor Decomposition. In *NIPS Workshop on Spectral Learning*. 4, 17, 25

MA, H., YANG, H., LYU, M.R. & KING, I. (2008). SoRec: social recommendation using probabilistic matrix factorization. In *Proceeding of the 17th ACM conference on Information and knowledge management*, CIKM '08, 931–940, ACM, New York, NY, USA. 52

MCCRAY, A. (2003). An upper-level ontology for the biomedical domain. *Comp Funct Genomics*, **4**, 80–4. 5, 66

MELACCI, S. & BELKIN, M. (2011). Laplacian Support Vector Machines Trained in the Primal. *Journal of Machine Learning Research*, **12**, 1149–1184. 81, 93, 94

MENON, A. & ELKAN, C. (2010). Predicting labels for dyadic data. *Data Mining and Knowledge Discovery*, **21**, 327–343. 82

MUGGLETON, S. & DE RAEDT, L. (1994). Inductive logic programming: Theory and methods. *The Journal of Logic Programming*, **19**, 629–679. 3

NEVILLE, J., RATTIGAN, M. & JENSEN, D. (2003). Statistical relational learning: Four claims and a survey. In *Proceedings of the Workshop on Learning Statistical Models from Relational Data, Eighteenth International Joint Conference on Artificial Intelligence*. 3

NG, M.K.P., LI, X. & YE, Y. (2011). MultiRank: co-ranking for objects and relations in multi-relational data. In *Proceedings of the 17th ACM SIGKDD international conference on Knowledge discovery and data mining*, KDD '11, 1217–1225, ACM, New York, NY, USA. 54

NICKEL, M. & TRESP, V. (2013). Logistic Tensor Factorization for Multi-Relational Data. In *Proceedings of the "Structured Learning: Inferring Graphs from Structured and Unstructured Inputs" Workshop (SLG 2013)*. 20, 25

NICKEL, M., TRESP, V. & KRIEGEL, H. (2011). A Three-Way Model for Collective Learning on Multi-Relational Data. In *Proceedings of the 2011 International Conference on Machine Learning (ICML)*. 4, 15, 25, 29, 35, 40, 52, 54, 63, 67, 102

NICKEL, M., TRESP, V. & KRIEGEL, H.P. (2012). Factorizing YAGO: scalable machine learning for linked data. In *Proceedings of the 21st international conference on World Wide Web*, WWW '12, 271–280, ACM, New York, NY, USA. 5, 52, 54

NIGAM, K., MCCALLUM, A. & MITCHELL, T. (2006). Semi-supervised text classification using EM. In O. Chapelle, B. Schölkopf & A. Zien, eds., *Semi-Supervised Learning*, 33–56, The MIT Press, Cambridge, MA. 81

OREN, E., GUÉRET, C. & SCHLOBACH, S. (2008). Anytime Query Answering in RDF through Evolutionary Algorithms. In *ISWC '08: Proceedings of the 7th International Conference on The Semantic Web*, 98–113, Springer-Verlag, Berlin, Heidelberg. 29

PRUD'HOMMEAUX, E. & SEABORNE, A. (2006). SPARQL Query Language for RDF. Tech. rep., W3C. 28, 29

RENDLE, S. & SCHMIDT-THIEME, L. (2010). Pairwise interaction tensor factorization for personalized tag recommendation. In *Proceedings of the third ACM international conference on Web search and data mining*, WSDM '10, 81–90, ACM, New York, NY, USA. 28, 29, 31, 33, 35, 36, 42

RENDLE, S., FREUDENTHALER, C., GANTNER, Z. & LARS, S.T. (2009a). BPR: Bayesian personalized ranking from implicit feedback. In *Proceedings of the Twenty-Fifth Conference on Uncertainty in Artificial Intelligence*, UAI '09, 452–461, AUAI Press, Arlington, Virginia, United States. 9, 20, 23, 24, 32, 35, 36, 60

RENDLE, S., MARINHO, L., NANOPOULOS, A. & SCHMIDT-THIEME, L. (2009b). Learning Optimal Ranking with Tensor Factorization for Tag Recommendation. In *Proceedings of the 15th ACM SIGKDD international conference on Knowledge discovery and data mining (KDD 2009)*, 727–736, ACM, New York, NY, USA. 23, 28

RENNIE, J. (2005). Smooth Hinge Classification. Tech. rep. 86

RICHARDSON, M. & DOMINGOS, P. (2006). Markov logic networks. *Machine learning*, **62**, 107–136. 3, 14

RUMMEL, R. (1999). *The Dimensionality of Nations Project: Attributes of Nations and Behavior of Nation Dyads, 1950-1965*. ICPSR (Series), Inter-University Consortium for Political & Social Research. 5, 66

SHEN, W., WANG, J., LUO, P. & WANG, M. (2012). LINDEN: linking named entities with knowledge base via semantic knowledge. In *Proceedings of the 21st international conference on World Wide Web*, WWW '12, 449–458, ACM, New York, NY, USA. 5

SIMSEKLI, U., ERMIS, B., CEMGIL, A.T. & ACAR, E. (2013). Optimal weight learning for coupled tensor factorization with mixed divergences. In *21st European Signal Processing Conference (EUSIPCO)* , EUSIPCO. 19, 24

SINGH, A.P. & GORDON, G.J. (2008a). A Unified View of Matrix Factorization Models. In *Proceedings of the European conference on Machine Learning and Knowledge Discovery in Databases - Part II*, 358–373, Springer-Verlag, Berlin, Heidelberg. 77

SINGH, A.P. & GORDON, G.J. (2008b). Relational learning via collective matrix factorization. In *Proceeding of the 14th ACM SIGKDD International Conference on Knowledge Discovery and Data Mining*, 650–658, ACM, New York, NY, USA. 4, 5, 15, 18, 19, 21, 25, 52, 53, 82, 85, 88

SINGH, A.P. & GORDON, G.J. (2010). A Bayesian matrix factorization model for relational data. In *Proceedings of the Annual Conference on Uncertainty in Artificial Intelligence (UAI)*. 4

SINTEK, M., GMBH, D. & DECKER, S. (2001). TRIPLE - An RDF Query, Inference, and Transformation Language. In *In Deductive Databases and Knowledge Management (DDLP 2001)*. 28

SUCHANEK, F.M., KASNECI, G. & WEIKUM, G. (2007). Yago: A Core of Semantic Knowledge. In *Proceedings of the 16th International Conference on World Wide Web*, WWW '07, 697–706, ACM, New York, NY, USA. 5

SZUMMER, M. & JAAKKOLA, T. (2002). Information regularization with partially labeled data. *Advances in Neural Information Processing Systems*, **15**, 1025–1032. 80

TAKEUCHI, K., ISHIGURO, K., KIMURA, A. & SAWADA, H. (2013). Non-negative multiple matrix factorization. In *Proceedings of the Twenty-Third international joint conference on Artificial Intelligence*, 1713–1720, AAAI Press. 4, 15

TANG, L. & LIU, H. (2009a). Relational learning via latent social dimensions. In *Proceedings of the 15th ACM SIGKDD International Conference on Knowledge Discovery and Data Mining KDD '09*, 817–826, ACM, New York, NY, USA. 67, 68, 69, 82

TANG, L. & LIU, H. (2009b). Scalable learning of collective behavior based on sparse social dimensions. In *Proceeding of the 18th ACM conference on Information and knowledge management*, CIKM '09, 1107–1116, ACM, New York, NY, USA. 68, 69

TUCKER, L. (1966). Some mathematical notes on three-mode factor analysis. *Psychometrika*, **31**, 297–311. 29

UDREA, O., SUBRAHMANIAN, V. & MAJKIC, Z. (2006). Probabilistic rdf. In *IEEE International Conference on Information Reuse and Integration*, 172–177, IEEE. 29

WANG, F., LI, T. & ZHANG, C. (2008). Semi-supervised clustering via matrix factorization. In *Proceedings of the 2008 SIAM International Conference on Data Mining*, 1–12, SIAM. 83

WEINBERGER, K., PACKER, B. & SAUL, L. (2005). Nonlinear dimensionality reduction by semidefinite programming and kernel matrix factorization. In *Proceedings of the Tenth International Workshop on Artificial Intelligence and Statistics*, 381–388. 83

XU, Z., TRESP, V., YU, K. & KRIEGEL, H.P. (2006). Infinite Hidden Relational Models. In *Proceedings of the 22nd International Conference on Uncertainity in Artificial Intelligence (UAI 2006)*, AUAI Press, Cambridge, MA, USA. 3

YANG, G. & KIFER, M. (2003). Reasoning about Anonymous Resources and Meta Statements on the Semantic Web. *J. Data Semantics*, **1**, 69–97. 28

YILMAZ, Y.K. (2012). *Generalized Tensor Factorization*. Ph.D. thesis. 19

ZHANG, Y., CAO, B. & YEUNG, D.Y. (2010). Multi-Domain Collaborative Filtering. In *Proceedings of the 26th Conference on Uncertainty in Artificial Intelligence (UAI)*, 725–732, Catalina Island, California. 52

ZHOU, D., BOUSQUET, O., LAL, T.N., WESTON, J. & SCHOLKOPF, B. (2004). Learning with local and global consistency. *Advances in Neural Information Processing Systems*, **16**, 321–328. 81, 93

ZHU, S., YU, K., CHI, Y. & GONG, Y. (2007). Combining content and link for classification using matrix factorization. In *Proceedings of the 30th annual international ACM SIGIR conference on Research and development in information retrieval*, SIGIR '07, 487–494, ACM, New York, NY, USA. 82

ZHU, X. (2008). Semi-supervised learning literature survey. Tech. Rep. 1530, University of Wisconsin, Madison. 80, 81

ZHU, X., GHAHRAMANI, Z. & LAFFERTY, J. (2003). Semi-Supervised Learning Using Gaussian Fields and Harmonic Functions. In *Proceedings of the Twentieth International Conference on Machine Learning (ICML)*, 912–919. 81, 94